MORNINGS FULL OF SUNLIGHT

a memoir

Elizabeth Driscoll

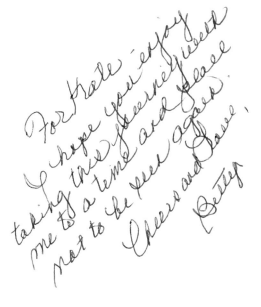

An imprint of Elizabeth Shanley Driscoll
esd1117@aol.com

Driscoll, Elizabeth
Mornings Full of Sunlight
ISBN 10: 0692262814
ISBN 13: 978-0692262818 (Elizabeth Shanley Driscoll)

... because lilacs smell sweet for such a short time, boys catch frogs and then let them go, and sisters picked berries on a warm sandy path a long time ago.

MORNINGS FULL OF SUNLIGHT

Obituary

Two columns of print in the *Philadelphia Inquirer,* December 10, 1981:

A five-alarm fire that started in the night ... Captain John Barry's house ... built in the early 1800s on the banks of the Delaware River ... purchased by the Religious of the Sacred Heart in 1847 ... a convent boarding school for more than a century. Eden Hall closed its doors in 1969 ... Flames shooting from the bell tower ... spread quickly in the wind ... chapel untouched by fire.

Polished pews gleam in predawn candlelight. Children kneel, veiled heads bowed in sleepy reverence. Shadows of statues pattern the walls and floor. Sisters with long, sweeping skirts and muffled steps move in and out of stalls beneath stained glass windows. Gregorian chant lingers in the stillness. A bell tolls, calling a small solitary figure from the outside world. The altar boy comes quickly, his red hair slicked flat across his freckled forehead, to dress in a long black cassock and white surplice that hang in the sacristy.

... Burned ... a fire of unknown origin ...

Incense rises from the sanctuary. We profess our faith in a universal language. We stand and sit and kneel as one, pews creaking and groaning with every move. The altar boy rings the bells. *Sanctus. Sanctus. Sanctus.* Slowly, silently, the nuns move towards the altar, exotic hooded crows. Their black veils fall forward, covering white wimples. We follow and kneel at the polished altar rail, mouths open like little birdlings waiting to be fed. The altar boy holds the golden plate in case the tiniest crumb falls.

Young and older voices blend in closing prayer. The altar boy snuffs the candle. His hair is dry. His bangs have fallen. A cowlick has sprung up.

... No one injured

Where are the students now? Did they read the news? Will they remember the feast days, the sea of white veils, the singing? Where are the nuns now? Who will tend the uniform white crosses and keep the iron gate painted— the altar boy? What about the grotto in the woods?

A fire makes us children again. Incense fills our senses, and smoke brings tears to our eyes. We listen for the chanting and the singing. We listen for the echo in our lives.

From the Beginning

Plates are passed at the dining room table. Sheer white curtains billow in and out of draperies. The air is fresh with spring, and the last of bird song is fading with the sun. Utensils clink on plates, chatter hums, and dinner proceeds as usual until my mother says she has exciting news. Knives and forks pause. My siblings and I exchange quick glances. All eyes are on the head of the table. Another baby?

My father announces that we are moving to a big house on ten acres in Rumson. The reaction is quick. "You're kidding!" More than possible, because my father often was.

I can tell by my mother's face it's true. Her eyes are twinkling like they do when she is happy. Her sister Anna and family moved to Rumson two years ago, and the seed had been planted. "You mean we are going to be living at the shore year round?"

The shore is the North Jersey Shore, where we have spent all our summers in a small town called Monmouth Beach. If you drive ten minutes north and cross the Sea Bright Bridge, a sign welcomes you to Rumson and lets you know that this town of stately old houses shaded by canopies of foliage was settled in 1665.

Voices fall on one another; questions and answers collide. The excitement is electric and flashes around the room, lighting up one face after another. Yes, we will still go to Monmouth Beach Club. Yes, once we are settled, we can get another dog.

We always had a dog, but the last one had not been replaced. Donnie, our cute, blond, cocker spaniel, had to go. We could not break him of an unfriendly habit he had of nipping at ankles. Nipping at ankles was our way of saying that this small dog attacked from the rear, and with pin sharp teeth grabbed at your Achilles, then ran off yelping as if he were the injured party. The last victim was Charles Kelly who, when he wasn't camped at our house, lived across the street. The dog ripped his sock and drew blood. Donnie had several last chances, but that was it. I didn't ask what happened to him because I really didn't want to know. I pictured him living with the three Bryce sisters who were kind, elderly sisters living in a small white cottage in Monmouth Beach and spent their days trimming flourishing rose bushes and playing bridge. They would certainly welcome the companionship of a dog, but more importantly they all had legs that went right into their shoes without the hint of an ankle.

Who wouldn't be excited at the prospect of living in a big white house on a hill with a long tree-lined driveway that leads to a porte-cochère? There are also a small cottage and a barn on the property. "No, no horses," my father says. We would be moving around the middle of June. The house has been vacant for quite a while; renovations are needed. Perfect, I think; school will be over, and we will be there for the summer—then I think again. "What about next year?"

Kitty, my oldest sister, will be starting college; Bobbie, the next oldest, will be a senior and will stay in South Orange and live with Grandma so she can graduate with her class. Betty (that's me) will go to Eden Hall. The two boys, Elliott and A.J., will attend Holy Cross Grammar School just a mile or two down the road.

Charlotte Anne, the baby, will stay home and take care of Mom.

"Wait a minute."

"Eden Hall? Eden Hall is a boarding school."

"Boarding school," my sisters laugh, and then they stop. Boarding school is no laughing matter. Orphans like Jane Eyre go to boarding school. Children from happy homes don't go to boarding school. I look at my dad and then at my mom. The words *boarding school* linger in my mouth like sour milk. I ask to be excused from the table. My mother glances at my full plate, hesitates, and then nods her permission. The room is silent as I depart.

By the time I reach the top of the stairs, the only thing on my mind is the dance on Saturday night. I phone Ceil to tell her about my dress and ask about hers.

Ceil and I were the only two freshmen at Marylawn who made the varsity basketball team, and we became best friends. We spent recess shooting around in the gym and went to practice together after school. On weekends we met up with the boys at the park and played basketball with them. Afterwards we walked to Grunnings in the Village, where we sipped Cokes and played the jukebox with the same boys we had challenged on the blacktop.

When I hear my sisters coming, I say good-bye. I don't mention moving to Ceil. Next year is a long way off.

Something will happen. Things will change, and I will not be going to boarding school.

Tree House

Our new house is big and beautiful, and all the things that make it home are already in place. The piano in the living room holds the same family pictures, the large portrait of a lady dressed in maroon velvet hangs over the fireplace. In the library my father's big, red leather chair stands in front of shelves filled with the same books with gilt-edged pages held tight between the same bookends that have guarded the stories I will read one day.

Kitty and I are sharing the bedroom on the left at the top of the stairs. I run up the stairs and stop in the doorway and try to take it all in. Four windows stretch from floor to ceiling, allowing sunlight to flood the green carpet and sending shadowed windowpanes up the far wall to frame blooming bouquets of lilacs on a pale green background. At the far end of the room a daybed sits in front of a fireplace framed by a white mantel. Our beds, bureaus, desk, and chair have already been arranged. I walk into our tree house and flop on the daybed. "Magic."

I watch Kitty's face when she appears in the doorway and scans the room. "Mine," I say, pointing to the bed with windows on both sides. She smiles, moves to her side of the room, and sits on the edge of the bed. "First come. First serve," I tease.

The last day of school was always the first day of summer. It didn't matter what the calendar said. We raced home to find the cars packed with just enough room for us to squeeze in the back. It was the same

7

every year as we headed to the beach for our longed-for summer vacation. I always wanted to ride in Dad's car. He led the way. I kept checking out the back window to make sure my mother's car was still following. I was also on the lookout for the moving van carrying our belongings: furniture, trunks, boxes, and most important, our bikes strapped to the back doors of the truck.

I learned to ride early, and from the day I rode out of my Father's 6'4" shadow into the sun while my sisters called "pedal and steer!" I went everywhere on that blue bike with balloon tires and silver bell. I rode up and down the sidewalk, in and out of driveways and, with permission, across the street. I gained immediate respect the day I rode over the sidewalk in front of Deanie Brown's house, where the roots of an old maple heaved concrete into a pyramid. When I bounced down on my balloon tires, I hurried back up the hill and tried it again and again.

The musty house always smelled good. Before the van had arrived, my brother and I were heading for the beach, kicking off our shoes, scampering across the sand, leaping over rows of broken shells as we raced to the water's edge.

A quick dash through freezing foam satisfied our longing and sent us back to still-damp sand to begin our castle. Using the biggest shells we could find, we dug and mounded, patted, smoothed, and drizzled sand. We scooped out tunnels, created a moat, and surrounded our masterpiece with shells bleached pure white by winter sun. While he carved and chiseled with a piece of driftwood, I searched for frosted sea glass, collected some black scallop shells, and found some smooth pink stones that would make this the best castle we ever built.

We worked while the sun fell behind us. Only when the smell of charcoal wakened our empty stomachs did we step back and admire our work, knowing that the sea would reclaim our creation.

That night I lay in bed and listened to the shade flapping against the window. The room smelled of Noxzema, and my skin felt too tight for my body.

The hot days of summer melt together in soft colors, but that first day remains sharp and clear. Summer means freedom, bare feet, and riding the waves.

Through the Back Door

Summer always ends before I am finished with it. We sit on the beach, our feet buried in the warm sand, watching a dark blue sea. Whitecaps rise and fall like miniature waves, moving sideways with the tide. The gulls huddle close to the sand.

I will be leaving for boarding school in the morning. Nothing has changed. My pleas have been heard, my arguments answered.

Yesterday's clear, crisp September weather is a memory. Heavy fog crept in while the house was sleeping. The window screen has trapped tiny orbs of moisture in its pores. Kitty is still asleep. I want to return to my dream, but the mourning doves keep crying.

I am dressed and ready to go too early. I go downstairs and sit in my father's big chair. He has already left for work. I am glad I don't have to say good-bye. By the time we depart, the sun is inhaling the fog and the temperature is rising.

I roll the window down, and a hot wind stings my eyes. My dark plaid cotton dress, chosen because it would travel well, is already stained with perspiration. I roll the window up. The radio exhales static. Kitty turns it off. The silence in the car grows louder.

I wonder why Kitty is coming. She will be leaving for college in a few days, and our tree house will be empty. We spent last night packing. The daybed was piled high with clothes that never found their way back into the closet. "Yours, yours, yours, mine ..." we sorted. Most of the clothes are hers. She is the shopper. I am the borrower.

The tires slap along the road. I crack the window, and the smell of tar fills the car. When we finally get off the highway and cross the bridge, we are on a two-lane road shaded by tall trees. Our speed is slower, and my sister rolls her window down.

Why am I going to boarding school? I never asked because it really didn't matter.

I never considered that my grandmothers, my mother, and her sisters all went to Sacred Heart schools. Katherine, just younger than my mother, had surprised everyone when she entered the convent. There were a few family trips during summers to visit her in her cloistered world. They were long trips by train and taxi. When we arrived at the heavy wooden door, Sister Portress welcomed us with a smile and a nod as we crossed the doorstep into this other world. We waited in a small parlor just to the left of the front door like a restless audience, sitting, standing, and changing seats until we heard the rustle of her robes, and then she was there framed in the doorway, eyes open wide in surprise, trying to take us all in at once. A laugh, too loud for a nun, especially one barely five feet tall, erupted as she rushed to greet us one by one, recalling our names before exchanging the traditional French air kisses, first one cheek and then the other. My father waited uncomfortably, his hat in his hand, until she finally reached him at the end of the line, where she simply held his hand in hers. "Elliott," she said looking up at his tall frame that saved him from the kisses.

After tea and sweets, known as goûter, we walked the grounds. While Mom and Katherine chatted, we ran ahead to investigate the statues and gardens and big shade trees, some perfect for climbing. A small playground with an empty jungle gym and swings seemed

to be waiting for the children who were gone for the
summer. Empty playgrounds always made me sad.

My father disappeared to smoke a cigarette. Mom
and Katherine sat on a bench while we pushed a merry-
go-round as fast as we could and dared each other to
jump off.

Am I being sacrificed in the name of tradition? I
never appealed to my father because, while he is the
provider and protector and usually has the last word,
my mother is the architect of our young lives. Her deci-
sions are made with good taste and for our own good.
They all laughed when I threatened to sit on my trunk
and light up a cigarette on my arrival. Somewhere deep
in my heart I know there must be some good reason I
am going to boarding school, but I can't think of any.

After more than two hours in the car, my mother says
we need to watch for Grant Avenue. We are in a neighborhood in northeast Philadelphia, where dark stucco
houses and empty driveways hide behind overgrown
rhododendrons. Two bikes collapsed and entangled in a
bush give the only hint that people inhabit these houses.
I know we are close, and my stomach feels like I just
stepped off the high dive.

Grant Avenue is a narrow, unlined road. We drive
along it until we arrive at two gray stone pillars support-
ing an open, black iron gate. EDEN is engraved on one
pillar, and HALL on the other. We enter slowly through
the narrow opening and more slowly up the long drive.
My dress peels off the seat as I lean forward to get a
better view.

A lush, green hockey field shaded by a line of leafy
oaks takes my mind off my dress. I roll the window down
and inhale the scent of newly cut grass baking in the sun.
Then, little by little, the rose-colored mansion begins to

emerge from the pine trees. We reach a circular drive, and the school looms in front of me. Long brown arms of fieldstone topped with multiple spires and crosses—rows of vacant windows stare back at me. I want to look away, but I can't. A tall dark figure standing at the top of the stairs waves us around to the rear of the building with her white handkerchief. I enter Eden Hall for the first time through the back door.

Down a narrow hallway leading to a wider corridor, a swarm of girls are greeting each other. I stop in the doorway, listening to their excitement.

"How was your summer?"

"Your hair looks *fabulous.*"

Because I can't penetrate the gaggle of girls, I stand in the doorway, my mother and sister behind me, and keep my eyes on the polished yellow floor patterned with sunlight beaming through a transom. Capezio shoes shuffle back and forth through the light: red ones, black ones, navy blue ones like mine. My shoes, I am sure, are the only things I have in common with these girls.

Finding my room seems like the safest thing to do, and although my mother suggests it would be proper to first greet Mother Benoist, the Mistress General, I ignore her and make my way across the hallway to the wooden staircase in search of Seven Dolors corridor, where the private rooms are located. I had insisted on a private room because I had never had a room of my own. But it was really because if I was going to be miserable, I was going to be miserable by myself.

Investigating several wrong hallways, we finally find my room, where my trunk has mysteriously arrived. Its black bulk fills the tiny dormered space, and I have to squeeze between it and the end of the bed to look out the casement window. From the second floor I look down on a courtyard shadowed by stone walls.

"No escape," I say, turning around to meet my mother's eyes. She smiles, but her eyes aren't twinkling. There is a pause, and I am afraid she is going to say something to comfort me, but instead she turns to the closet. She is always concerned about closet space. Six hangers await the two wool jumpers—navy blue for daytime, plaid for evening—and a white dress for Sunday, along with three white blouses that she begins hanging up. A nun with a kind voice comes by and advises me that my worldly clothing will be kept in a community closet on the third floor and can be retrieved the night before vacation or an outing. Outing? What is an outing? I wonder. My nightclothes should be folded neatly and kept under my pillow. She shows us where the bathroom is and explains a schedule for showering. There is another schedule for the bathtubs that are located down another hall. We unpack my trunk and deliver my clothes to the students' community closet.

Mother Benoist welcomes us warmly as Mother McDonnell's family. Katherine and Mother Benoist had been in the novitiate together at Kenwood. While my mother seats herself next to Mother Benoist on a sofa, Kitty and I sit down across from them on antique chairs that have been made to suit a shorter generation. Our knees rise above what would normally be a lap. I look at her and roll my eyes as she tries to arrange her feet in a ladylike manner. From the conversation I learn that a classmate of my mother's, Mother Carmody, will be my English teacher. I am relieved when our visit ends, and we escape without anything being spilled or shattered. We follow each other to the study hall and find my desk among rows of like ones. Mother Carmody meets us in the doorway. She is taller and thinner than any of the other nuns, and she blushes when my Mother calls her Mary Louise. The usual French greeting that follows is awkward if not comical due to the fact that my mother is at least half a foot shorter. By the time I am introduced to Mother Carmody, her blush is in full bloom as she welcomes me.

While they chat, Kitty and I slip into the hallway. "Write when you can," she says.

"You too."

I notice the patch of sunlight is gone.

"You better get going. Mom doesn't like to drive in the dark."

I walk with them to the front door. "You'll be all right," my mother says.

I am not sure if it is a question or some kind of assurance. I see tears gathering in her eyes, and I nod my head.

"Write," Kitty says again.

"I will, I will."

I close the door behind them.

Congé. Goûter. Feast day. *Primes. Surveillante.* Mistress General. Reverend Mother. Mother General. There is no orientation; I am absorbed into ranks, assimilated into a routine.

Mother Forden, Mother Benoist, Mother Stuart, Mother Hupp: will I ever be able to tell them apart? Faces encircled by white wimples draped in black veils move silently in and out of a maze of corridors. Only Mother Carmody stands out.

It is Mother Forden who swoops into the study hall and calls us to attention with a wooden clapper hidden in her hand. We receive instructions for the rest of the evening. The invisible clapper sounds again. I follow a horde of girls down the stairs to the refectory, up the stairs to the gym, down the chapel corridor, back to the study hall, and finally a bell that sends us to our rooms. I have twenty minutes to get ready for bed before the next bell signals lights out. I feel safer in the darkness than I have felt all day. Alone with the thin line of light under my door, I strain for the sounds of Nanny's radio.

Mornings Full of Sunlight

A, my name is Alice
And my husband's name is Alfred

Airmail letters came addressed to Alice Reeves, but her real name was Nanny, and she didn't have a husband. She came from England to take care of new babies. She took care of my sisters before I was born. Her hair was as white as her starched uniform. She fell one night and hit her head on the radiator. Blood soaked red through her soft curls. My father took her to the hospital. I closed my eyes tight and tried to say my prayers. I could still see circles of thick red blood inside my eyelids. When morning came, Nanny was there beside my bed. She showed me her clean white bandage.

Red sun in the morning, sailors take warning.
Red sun at night, sailors delight.

I never really understood the meaning, but I liked the sound of the words and the mystery in Nanny's voice.

I was no longer able to see her face, but one morning when I was pulling the white sheets tight and smoothing the wrinkles with the palm of my hand, her face was there just for a moment. The pictures in the albums show a younger Nanny leaning over the English pram.

Mornings were full of sunlight. Nanny hovered around my bed, patting my blanket and whispering, "Time to get up." At night there was a thin line of light under my door and the sound of Nanny's radio.

Nanny didn't play cards. It was against her religion. She had ridges in her fingernails. If I took my tonic, I wouldn't get ridges.

Once, Nanny left to take care of another family's baby. She packed up all her belongings in a small black suitcase but left her radio and a promise to come back.

Ride a cockhorse to Banbury Cross
To see a fine lady upon a white horse.
Rings on her fingers and bells on her toes
She shall have music wherever she goes.

She was holding our new baby on her lap the day of the May procession. I don't remember whose idea it was, but a group of us spent the morning converting our backyard into a chapel. We ran back and forth gathering flowers, candles, crepe paper, and ribbon. My older sister turned an old green wicker table into an altar with a white tablecloth and a package of thumbtacks. Lilacs were stuffed into glass jars, and the statue of the Blessed Mother stood between them. Susan and I collected lawn chairs from neighbors' garages and porches and arranged them in pew-like rows.

The pews were filled with the faithful: mothers in cotton dresses, fathers in golf shirts, and Nanny in starched white. Deanie Brown and Dickey Crummy sat cross-legged on the ground in front of her with their baseball gloves resting in their laps.

We filed slowly around the backyard. I was carrying a tiny crown of twisted violets on a satin baby pillow. I kept my eyes on the feet in front of me, not daring to raise them. My white gloves grew damp as we continued at a snail's pace. Our weak voices were joined by the faithful in the pews. "Oh Mary we crown thee with blossoms today." Karen climbed onto the milk box covered with blue crepe paper and lifted the wilting crown. The singing had stopped, and so had the birds. Somewhere in my chest a breath waited. As late afternoon sun patterned our backyard chapel, Karen placed the crown on Mary's head.

Everyone knelt. Mary Anne knelt on a thumbtack. A great fuss was made over the tiniest red hole in her knee.

That night I lay in the dark, listening to sleeping noises coming from my sister's bed. It was raining, or dripping, as Nanny would say. I got up and went to the window. It was dark, but I could still see the altar covered with the tablecloth. I smelled lilacs, and I heard Nanny saying, "Lovely, just lovely."

I was thirteen when I went away to boarding school. When I came home, Nanny was gone, gone to a nursing home. They said she was old and couldn't take care of babies anymore. My sister brought her home for a visit. When I saw the car coming up the driveway, I ran to greet her. She was so small I could only see the top of her head through the window. I leaned in and kissed her hair; her scalp was pink like a baby's.

Grass Never Grew in Our Yard

"Have you met Cynthia?" someone asks excitedly. I am a ship sinking in a sea of strange voices, when I realize that the tall girl with the short black hair is smiling at me. "Cynthia?" I manage to reply. Cynthia is a new student beginning her second year of high school at Eden Hall. We will be classmates in the Second Academic. I've been thrown a lifeline. I will have something in common with her.

Then the same girl tells me that Cynthia is the daughter of the famous British actor, Basil Rathbone, and that she and her parents had arrived today in a limousine. I wonder if a nun with a white handkerchief waved them around to the back door.

As I stand behind my chair at dinner that night waiting for a small silver bell to signal the blessing before meals, I scan the refectory and wonder which of the many unknown faces might be Cynthia.

A full day passes before Cynthia and I actually connect. At morning Mass she crumples against me, pinning me to the pew. Mother Fordan swoops to the rescue with smelling salts. When we come out of the chapel, Cynthia is sitting alone in the hallway. Afraid to break ranks, I file right past her. Later, on the way to Mother Carmody's class, I catch up with her and ask if she is okay. She smiles and says she is. Cynthia has already suffered the embarrassment of her mother packing undershirts in her trunk, a fact that traveled through the student body almost as fast as she stashed them in the back of her drawer and laughed it off. I take the seat across the aisle from her in class, and while my eyes are fastened on Mother Carmody standing stick tall with her hands clasped below her waist, I am aware of Cynthia sitting tall in her chair, pen poised over the sheet of paper that smells like purple ink and is still warm off the machine. If she feels ill or embarrassed, there is no sign. I resist picking up my paper to smell the fresh ink. During the class I focus on learning the names of some of my classmates. Yvonne is the tall girl with the short black hair and the big smile. I fall in step with her on the way to our next class. She heard I was from New Jersey. We sit together in the back of the room during history class. I wonder if we will be friends.

Cynthia is at the next table at lunch. She is smiling and talking with her tablemates.

Hurry! Classes are over. We change into red tunics, grab our hockey sticks from our lockers and then our *goûter* from a large rectangular tray of brownies, and head for the field. Cynthia and I are assigned to a small group of girls who are new to the sport. We gather on the upper field and are instructed in the art of "stick work" by one of the varsity players. Cynthia and I are equally inept and form a partnership to practice passing and driving. We do a lot of laughing and chasing balls. I can hear the athletes on the other field cracking the ball. I have inherited my father's athletic genes, and as far back as second grade, I realized that I was one of the lucky ones who could run and throw and swing with ease. I was playing baseball in our front yard on Berkeley Avenue when these good players were dribbling, passing, and shooting a hockey ball. Everyone in the neighborhood played baseball at our house. Grass never grew in our yard.

I *was eight when we moved to Berkeley Avenue. It was easy to make friends then; easy, comfortable friendships formed because you were the same age, went to the same school, or just liked to jump rope.*

Betsey Ferris and I were bosom buddies, friends forever. Our friendship survived different schools, the same boyfriend, and rooting for different baseball teams.

If you grew up in New Jersey during the 1950s, you weren't just a fan, you were a New York Yankee or a Brooklyn Dodger. I wore a shiny blue jacket with white letters that proclaimed my Dodger loyalty. Betsey had a baseball signed by Yogi Berra.

But baseball wasn't just Ebbets Field or Yankee Stadium. You could hear calls of "Steerike!" and "Out!" rise from behind the rhododendron bushes that surrounded our yard. From the tree stump to the brick path to home, we imitated our flannel heroes. We knew their batting averages, collected and flipped their cards, copied their batting stances, and called each other by their nicknames: Pee Wee, Campy, Joe D., and Scooter.

Almost every afternoon and all day Saturday you could find most of the neighborhood at our house. We chose teams, made the rules, and settled our own disputes. If there weren't enough players, we made up games: "one strike, three shoot," "fly catchers up," or "hit the bat." Betsey's lawn was perfect. Her father spent Saturdays edging flower gardens, raking grass, or pruning trees. A huge rope hammock hung between two apple trees. When I wasn't playing baseball, we would lie in that hammock, squinting at patches of blue sky between the leaves. If we swung the hammock high enough, we could pick apples right off the tree.

Even though she was a baseball fan, Betsey didn't play baseball. I guessed she didn't have the genes.

On a warm September day in 1951, I sat in my father's brand new Studebaker, listening for the third out. He had gone inside to watch the end of the Dodgers vs. Giants game on television. The Dodgers were comfortably on their way to another pennant, but the Giants came on strong as the season was coming to a close. The last game between the Dodgers and Giants would determine the National League champs. The sun was on its way down and glinted off the windshield. I sat in the front seat of my father's car and prayed for the third out. The neighborhood was silent. The other kids had wandered off, and my father had gone inside. The voice of Russ Hodges floated out of the car into the stillness of the neighborhood. Bobby Thompson came to the plate while I pleaded with the pitcher, "Throw strikes." I heard the crack of the bat and the instantaneous roar of the crowd and then the cry: "The Giants win the pennant! The Giants win the pennant! The Giants win the pennant!"

The words followed me across the backyard and up the stairs to my room. There would be no Yankee/Dodger World Series this year.

Betsey never mentioned the game. That's how it was with best friends.

One of the hard things about growing up is leaving friendships behind. I wonder whatever happened to Betsey Ferris and to my silky blue Dodger jacket.

Cynthia and I are on our way to the hockey field later that week. We are passing the statue of Saint Michael, and Cynthia says something about a saint with a sword and then, in the most offhanded way, she tells me that she isn't Catholic.

"You're not Catholic? Why did your parents send you to a convent boarding school?" I blurt out. She begins to explain about her parents traveling between New York and California for her father's work and how changing schools was difficult and boarding school seemed a good idea.

"But why a convent boarding school?"

A whistle signals we are late. Cynthia is saying something about a good education and values as we run. I picture her kneeling in an empty pew in the chapel while everyone else in the chapel is filing to the altar to receive communion. How could her parents do that to her? Wasn't it hard enough being the new girl and trying to find your place? Cynthia begins every day by being excluded. How does she feel kneeling there all alone surrounded by empty pews, waiting to be part of the student body again? What do the other students think? Her courage, if that's what it is called, diminishes my own. I want to be accepted, to be part of the whole.

For the next hour we race the ball and each other up and down the field under a clear sky. My lungs fill with fresh air, and my strides lengthen and become fluid. I will never have the skills of the others, but I enjoy the striving.

The sun is weak now; I walk slowly behind the others, reluctant to give up the outdoors. I pull the fresh air into my lungs and kick my way through the brown leaves.

My sisters and I used to rake all the leaves into a giant pile. Then we would pump the swing as high as we could and jump off into the pile of leaves. This was as close to flying as I ever came except in my dreams.

Maybe an only child like Cynthia looked forward to going to boarding school.

The Student Body

The wooden clapper brings us to attention and then to ranks. We are the student body: a mass of blue wool uniforms, starched white blouses, and stiff white veils. From tallest to shortest we pass along the chapel corridor. It is dark when we enter the chapel, but now as we exit, singing, "Are we not thy chosen soldiers, children of the Sacred Heart?" the sun is rising, striping the yellow wood floor that shines under years of wax and constant polish. We move out of the chapel and into the day. Back in the study hall, we stash our veils and our reverence in desks that stand two by two in long, solemn rows. Desktops are lifted and dropped with machine gun cadence. Mother Fordan dismisses us with a frown, and another ritual begins.

While the student body moves down the wide wooden staircase to the refectory, where hot chocolate is already steaming in enamel pots, the "squad" (hockey team) and "dieters" head outside for the track.

The track is actually a cinder path that runs by the stone barn and the house where Mr. Mooney, the caretaker, lives with his wife and six redheaded children. Mr. Mooney is the only male on the property besides his young sons, who come to the chapel each morning to serve as altar boys. From behind his house the path winds down a slight incline past the grotto and the cemetery, where even rows of clean white crosses are enclosed by a black iron fence. It is here that the nuns will be buried after living out their lives, faithful to their vows even in death. From this, the farthest point on the edge of the property, the path winds back to the main building alongside an empty field that in the old days yielded seasonal crops.

I grab my sweater. It is a sunny October morning, but I know it will be cold. It is always cold at this early hour. I shoulder my way out the door, pulling my sweater over my head. My body recoils at the initial slap of fresh air, and the cold pinches my nose. I am the first one out. I like to be first, and I like to run alone. I follow my breath to the path. My shoulders are tight, and my stride is short as I begin. No one else is on the track yet. They'll be coming soon in twos and threes, hockey players first, dieters walking behind. I breathe through my nose, trying to stave off the inevitable pain I know will seize my throat, but I can't get enough oxygen. I try to siphon a shallow breath or two through the corner of my mouth. I inhale once, and the pain is already there, yanking on my windpipe. I try cupping my mouth in my hands to trap the warmth of my breath, but that's no help. The others are coming now. I swallow the pain and pick up my pace. Some initial shouts of "Hurry up!" and "Where's Kate?" are quickly silenced by the cold. Now we suffer together. We are the team, a squad of warriors ready to do battle on Friday. A band of gladiators dressed in red tunics, we'll take to the field amid chants of victory. There will be no pain then. We leave our pain on the cinder path.

My stride has lengthened, and I move more easily. Heel, toe, heel, toe, heel, toe, my hair is lifting and falling on my shoulders. I fall into a comfortable rhythm, which carries me around the curve.

I am back in Miss Renée's ballet class. Her shrill voice carried my eight-year-old body across the studio floor. One, two, three, leap. One, two, three, leap. I ran

and soared before Miss Renée could sa
what was coming, and I could not hol
was soaring—the thrill of the lift, the
pension, the touch. Again and again I tc

The sun is on my back now. My legs l   ...
to the grotto, halfway around the track and far enough
ahead of the others to slow down here in the hollow
and let the pain in my throat subside, then past the neat
white crosses, and back along the edge of the empty
field. My windpipe must surely be lined with ice and
ready to crack. Some days the pain eases before I reach
the end and is gone by the time I turn onto the macadam
drive and head for the finish. Not today. I am breathing
through the woolen sleeve of my sweater as I slow to a
jog and stagger to a stop. I am first.

Inside the door, I pause for a moment to enjoy the
spartan pleasure until the smell of hot chocolate lures me
to the refectory. The students who don't run are already
seated at the round tables that fill the square room.

"*Bonjour, ma mère.*"

"*Bonjour,*" she smiles and nods as she walks around
the room, her hands tucked deep in her sleeves. I slip
into my empty seat and turn my cup up. Sister comes im-
mediately and fills it from a blue speckled kettle that is
almost as big as she is. The brown liquid swirls into the
cup, and I lift it with two hands and inhale the steam.

The others are coming now with red noses and tight
lips, carrying the scent of cold air into the room as they
fill the remaining empty places at the circular tables.
Like pieces of pie, they fill the circle. We are roommates
and desk mates and classmates and teammates. We are
the student body.

Mysterium Tremendum

Everyone remembers her first grade teacher. Sister Ann Phillip was mine. She was not much bigger than a fourth grader. Her robes swept the linoleum floor as she moved up and down the short aisles checking our penmanship. The first and second grades at Marylawn shared the same classroom and Sister Ann Phillip. Seventeen of us sat in four rows of wooden desks that stretched like the blackboard from one side of the room to the other. One day, Sister Ann Phillip's rosary beads caught on the corner of Billy Riley's desk. I watched in horror as they broke apart, and three Hail Marys bounced across the floor.

When I looked up at her red face pinched behind the square white frame, I expected to see her make a hurried sign of the cross or hear a whispered "Jesus, Mary, and Joseph," but she just stood there fingering the broken strand. Then she walked to the front of the room, picked up the errant black beads, and held them in the palm of her hand before sending them tumbling through the darkness of her deep pocket that periodically produced gold-trimmed holy cards of angels in flowing pink with transparent wings. One day my yellow yo-yo went into that pocket and never came out.

After recess Sister Ann Phillip held the arched door open, and we filed in below her big black wing. It was hard to come in from air and sky and sun and adjust to walls, ceilings, and forced heat. The rhythm of the jump rope slapping the driveway and the words of "Fudge, fudge, tell the judge" were still ringing in my ears. I brushed against the soft cloth of her skirt, feeling for the wounded beads. Back in the classroom, I watched carefully as she made her way to the blackboard, straining to catch a glint of the silver cross that hung on the end of her beads. Had that, too, gone into her pocket? Would Sister Ann Phillip pull a whole rosary out of that mysterious pocket and hold it high for all of us to see? She told us stories about saints and miracles.

Before school, catechism class, miracles, or Sister Ann Phillip, I knew about my soul. I knew that it sat on my right shoulder like an epaulet, was made of pure white satin, and was easily stained by "thoughts, words, deeds, and omissions." I knew all this because I had two older sisters, and I asked a lot of questions. My theological research was often stymied by "go to sleep," but I filled in the blanks and formed my own creed. Venial sins left tiny black pinholes on my white satin soul, but mortal sins left black scabby marks that could cause gangrene. If you died with gangrene, you couldn't go to heaven.

Because I already had little black marks on my soul, I was relieved when Sister Ann Phillip taught us about the Sacrament of Penance. I could tell my sins to the priest in confession, and for three Hail Marys, two Our Fathers, and a good Act of Contrition, I could get my sins erased. It was like sending your soul to the dry cleaners. Before we could make our first communion, we would make our first confession. Waiting my turn to enter the little room where Father Sullivan sat behind a screen covered with a white linen cloth that looked like the ones Grandma had in her powder room, I went over my sins and the things necessary to gain absolution. I must confess my sins, be truly sorry, and make a firm purpose of amendment. "Bless me Father, for I have sinned." It began easily. I had told some lies, fought with my brother and sisters, talked back to my mother, and taken some quarters from her pocketbook. The difficult part *would be how many times. How many lies had I told in my life? How many times had I fought with my sisters? Five? Ten? Fifty? I knew how many times I had taken quarters from my mother's pocketbook: once when she left it sitting on a chair in the hallway, and another time when her red leather change purse was on her dressing table. The real problem came when Father Sullivan asked if I had made reparation for my sins. I wasn't sure what reparation meant, but I quickly answered, "Yes." His next question clarified the first. "You put the money back?" "Yes, Father," I lied. How could I tell him about my new tin bank that stuck out its tongue and swallowed those quarters, and how the disappearing coins clanked into the bottom of the clown's stomach? I hesitated before closing the door to the confession room slowly. Should I go back in? Confess again? The next person was coming, too late.*

I went to bed that night with a troubled mind and a dirty soul. "Are you awake?" I asked my sister. She said I shouldn't worry. There would be confession again next week.

Any worries I had disappeared on the playground. The first to cross the finish line was the winner. Three strikes and you're out. If you missed on your turn at jump rope, you went to the end of the line. The rules were black and white. I could jump double Dutch and hot pepper. I was always one of the first to be picked for a team. Although reading and math came easily to me, nothing felt as natural as running and jumping and throwing. Little worried me in first grade besides confession. As far as that yellow yo-yo went, I firmly believed that someday that deep, dark pocket would cough it up.

It wasn't until second grade that I heard about a permanent record.

What Is a Permanent Record?
(And Where Is Kingdom Come, Anyway?)

A permanent record is a yellow, dog-eared card where all your deeds and misdeeds were recorded while you were a student at Marylawn School of the Oranges. There was a card for every student who ever attended the school. Hundreds and hundreds of cards were stored in long black and white cardboard boxes, just like the covers of our composition books, and hidden somewhere in the bowels of the building. Only one or two people, not even Sister Ann Phillip, knew the exact location.

We all heard the story about one of Marylawn's students applying for a job with the government. The FBI came to Marylawn to check his permanent record. I think he got the job.

I was still not sure where "Kingdom Come" was. Dickey Crummy's mother said that if he walked in the house again with mud on his shoes, she was going to knock him into "Kingdom Come."

Mail Call

In a matter of weeks, I master a maze of hallways, decipher the system of bells, figure out the chain of command, and learn how to curtsy on the run. At Eden Hall we curtsy to Reverend Mother Ashe, who stands at the top of the hierarchy of nuns, and to the Mistress General, Mother Benoist, who is second in command. Without any signs of embarrassment, Sacred Heart girls dip gracefully while in full stride, passing Reverend Mother in the hallway or passing Mother Benoist's office, which opens onto the main hallway. Sometimes we curtsy to an empty office as we hurry to the gym. I practice my curtsy in front of the only big mirror in the school, in the downstairs lavatory, until I am gliding easily across the black and white tiles.

Our days move forward on a relentless schedule. Every day begins and ends the same. Every week copies the one before it: Religion/Literature/History/Latin and, never soon enough, lunch and mail call!

After the Angelus rings and we pray, the sisters wheel out the carts and distribute the blue and white lunch platters; we fill our plates, and the eating and chatter begin. I keep one eye on the open double doors where Mother Benoist will soon appear, cradling the brown basket in her right arm. Today it is overflowing with mail, and my expectations rise. She stops in the doorway. Her thin red face barely parts the white wimple, and her small dark eyes dart about the room, searching for the person who will have the honor of distributing the mail today. She heads to the far side of the refectory, where Loli is taken by surprise.

"Me, Mother? Are you sure, Mother?" Loli is large and loud and usually in trouble for one thing or another. Laughter and sporadic applause break out and even a smile from Mother Benoist. Loli delivers the mail with flair. A letter and two postcards make my day. My table-mates are impressed that the postcards are from the University of Notre Dame. I don't tell them they are from my sister's boyfriend and his roommate. I warned everyone that the mail was censored. George and Johnny didn't seem to care. I hope the censor had a sense of humor. I notice the envelope in my hand is slit only half open.

Who had time to read all these letters? Of course no one did. I shouldn't have been surprised.

When I tear open the rest of the envelope and re-move the stationery, something that resembles a squir-rel's tail slips into my lap. I cover it with my napkin and avoid looking at my tablemates as I read the tale of the tail, a story that will be told and retold over the years like so many others that we know by heart but continue to tell because they makes us laugh.

John and a few of his friends had been hunting squir-rels in the woods next to his house. One of them shot a squirrel and then propped the still warm body between the branches of a large evergreen. When Rick arrived late, someone handed him a shotgun and pointed out the squirrel. He took quick aim and fired. "Bull's-eye!" someone yelled. "What a shot!" "Wow," said Rick, "it never even moved!"

I shove the tail in my blazer, thankful that this stiff piece of fur hadn't surprised Mother Benoist. When lunch is over, I hurry out of the refectory to avoid questions and catch up with Yvonne. On the way to class I tell her I got a love letter and show her what is in my pocket. "Give it," she says. I know she is thinking about having some fun with it. I smile and then think again. The tail remains in my pocket.

Algebra/Logic/Chemistry/*Goûte*/Sports

Classes drag on. Is it because math and chemistry are my least favorite subjects or because of the tail in my pocket? The windows are open in chemistry class, and I consider ... but we are on the second floor ... someone might see it in flight.

A quick change into my red tunic, black tights, and cleats, and I am off to the lower field. I grab a square of cake with chocolate icing off one of the long trays, tuck my hockey stick under my arm, and run. The fields are still lush and green. Orange and yellow leaves have gathered in the back of the goal, where a brisk breeze must have whipped them. The air is cool, the sun is warm, and I have graduated from the beginners' field to the big field. I love racing the ball in my wing position. I head for the goal and drive the white ball just past the goal into a pile of leaves. In one quick move I retrieve the ball and dispose of the tail.

The fresh air is exhilarating, and practice flies by. I am not ready to go back inside, so I walk slowly across the field and back up to the driveway. Everything is still. I linger in the last rays of sun that has washed everything in gold. It is five o'clock in the afternoon—that golden time of day.

The tower clock strikes. I'm late again? Running up the steps to the second floor, I am ripping the belt off my red tunic when Yvonne passes me on her way down. She laughs and calls from below. "Hurry."

41

Dinner/Free Time/Study Hall

Mashed potatoes again?

"Don't eat the mashed potatoes," I was warned the first week. "They put saltpeter in them." Saltpeter, someone explained, is a white powder that helps to calm the libido. I wasn't at all sure this was true and figured they might just be having fun with the new girl. Over the next few months I watched bowl after bowl of untouched mashed potatoes return to the kitchen. Could tonight's potatoes be the same ones we sent back last night?

Some nights I go to the chapel after dinner. It is dark. A few candles in front of the statues send shadows moving on the walls. I like being alone in the silence. I think and pray and listen for some movement in the choir loft over the visitor's chapel. I know the sounds of the solemn pipes are about to begin. Her eyes are weak and her balance is unsteady, but seated at the organ her hands and feet move automatically, and the sounds of the organ are strong and resolute. When she stops I hope she will begin again, but she never does. Her sacred music is all of a piece, one continuous hymn of praise. I imagine her struggling down the narrow stairs and shuffling away. Like the music, she comes and goes from an unknown place and then disappears into the dark recesses of the convent.

The study hall is quiet. There are lots of empty desks tonight because they are having tryouts for Glee Club. I think about the letter from John and imagine the fun they had and am happy that they included me in it. I rest my head in my folded arms on top of the open pages of my literature book. Music escapes from the parlor as the singers return one by one. The wall clock whines and clicks into place.

We end our day as we started it, on our knees.

Counting By Threes

I *was born the third child and the third girl in our family, and it never occurred to me that I might have been a disappointment to my father. When I was four, my brother was born and people were slapping my father on the back, saying, "At last!" and "Congratulations!" Even then I did not imagine that I was not the most wanted and loved child.*

I liked being the third girl. There were footsteps to follow. I knew at five I would go to Miss Beard's School. The next year I would go to first grade at Marylawn. My teacher would be Sister Ann Phillip. You can learn a lot just by tagging along with your older sisters.

"One, two, three, breathe. One, two, three, breathe," Mr. Wells would call as Kitty and Bobbie went back and forth across the pool, holding on to the blue kickboards, kicking and breathing on cue. When they put the kickboards aside to do stroke work, I would take one of them to the baby pool and practice. Each time they took a lesson, I was there watching and listening. By the end of the summer my sisters were strong swimmers. My mother said it was my turn to have lessons. "I don't need lessons," I told her. "I already know how. Watch me."

"Watch me, watch me!" I called again and again to make sure my mother wouldn't loose track of me in the crowded baby pool.

I buried my head in the water, pushed off the side of the pool, and kicked and pulled until I touched the other side. While I was wiping the water out of my eyes, I heard my mother calling to my sisters to come see. "Do it again!" my sisters urged. I never refused them. They were my favorite audience.

Taking a big gulp of air, I fought my way this time from one end of the pool to the other. Before I had gotten halfway, my arms felt heavy and my feet began to sink. I fought to keep them moving. "One, two, three, breathe." I couldn't get my head out of the water, but I could see the wall underwater. I kicked and reached, and when I finally touched I was gasping and choking, water pouring out of my nose as I tried to suck air back into my lungs. I heard my sisters laughing and clapping.

"Now you can swim in the big pool!" they called.

"Not so fast," my mother laughed and wrapped me in a towel.

I still love making my sisters laugh, but my mother's laugh lies just beyond my hearing.

First Communion

Morning's white light, a gentle breeze ...
Everything ready and waiting ...
Dress, veil, shoes ... waiting ...

Altar rail draped in white satin ...
Trumpeting lilies and lilies of the valley ...
Billy Riley kneeling next to me in his new white suit,
His round, freckled face polished to a shine.

Father Sullivan robed in white vestments ...
Everything white and waiting ...

Sister Ann Phillip kneeling close by ...
We are ready and waiting
To be called to the altar of God.

First communions were celebrated, like other important occasions, at my grandmother's perfect house at the
end of the lane. The huge foyer with the parquet floor
was my stage. I twirled and leaped and grew up on that
stage until it became a ballroom. After brunch in the
dining room my sisters and I played hide and seek in the
rose garden while the grown-ups sipped coffee on the
terrace. Tomorrow Mr. Murphy would rake the white
stones into place.

Life was so certain at seven.

When we arrived home, I skipped down the hill
to show my friend Anne my dress and the thin gold

45

bracelet my grandmother gave me. She met me before I got halfway down the hill. I heard her call, "The President is dead!" I stopped and stared. "Don't you know? The President is dead."

I walked back home, careful not to step on any cracks. My father's head bent close to the radio told me it was true. I went upstairs, took off my dress, and hung it in the closet.

That night my sisters tented the space between the beds with blankets, and we listened undercover to the radio. We kept it very low (Rinso white, Rinso bright, happy little wash day song), and when we heard my mother coming down the hall to kiss us goodnight, we turned it off.

I lay awake long after my sisters had fallen asleep. The streetlight was shining in the window, and I could see my dress hanging in the closet. I waited to hear my father's footsteps coming up the stairs, but sleep came before he did.

The next morning big black headlines filled the small white kitchen: "FDR DEAD." My father was behind the paper, and everyone was moving quietly. The milkman came and went without a greeting. The clank of empty milk bottles was my only assurance that life was proceeding outside. I wished I could stay home and sit in the warm patch of sunlight on the carpet in my mother's room and listen to the sound of her voice in the empty neighborhood.

"Come on," my sisters called as the screened door slammed. I turned to say good-bye to my father. He was still behind the headlines.

Primes

The Religious of the Sacred Heart, also referred to as the Madams or Ladies of the Sacred Heart, were, as Mary McCarthy says in *Memories of a Catholic Girlhood*, "not *ordinary* nuns." They came from the best families, were educated at the best schools, and there was a sense of aristocracy present in everything they did. Their schools followed a pattern laid down for them in France in the early nineteenth century. The institutions they founded to educate young women were "clipped and pollard as a garden and stately as a minuet."

The elegant refinement that surrounds me passes unnoticed. I am too busy trying to find my way, beginning a new life in a foreign place. I am on my own. I am often in the wrong place, out of uniform because I rolled up my sleeves, and seemingly late for everything.

Monday mornings begin with *Primes* (prizes). Under Mother Forden's sharp eye, we rearrange the study hall, pushing the desks aside and placing the chairs in three rows of one large semicircle. Then we put on our white gloves, straighten our stockings, brush off the shoulders of our navy blue blazers, and stand at attention while Reverend Mother and a bevy of black robes begin collecting in the hall, hovering just outside and then flocking into the room, settling on their chairs and adjusting their feathers. Reverend Mother sits in an armchair on a raised platform. Mother Forden stands on the left side of the community, facing the student body, prepared to read from a large black notebook. "Fourth Academic, all very good." The students, already positioned in front of the community, move forward from the middle of the semicircle. They curtsy as each one accepts a small blue card bearing the Sacred Heart insignia and inscribed with the words "*Très Bien.*" Very Good means that you have conducted yourself throughout the week with all the charms and graces expected of a Sacred Heart girl while observing the rules and regulations.

The Third Academic stands on cue and takes their place. The procedure is repeated class after class, unless some infraction has been recorded.

"Second Academic, all very good *except* ..." The word *except* catches everyone's attention "... Elizabeth Shanley for violating dormitory rules." My heart's pumping blood to my face.

I know to take a step back while the "Very Goods" pass in front of me to receive their commendations. I fall to the end of the line and follow at a respectful distance to receive a brown card from Reverend Mother's deathly white hand. I curtsy, apologize, and return to my seat. My cheeks are burning. I swallow hard to hold back tears.

The infraction was breaking dormitory rules? I remember that on Saturday we had a late sleep, an extra half hour before the big bell shook us from our narrow beds. I was taking my time getting dressed, enjoying the leisure of stretching and yawning. Before I knew it, the warning bell had rung and I was late. I pulled on my uniform, tied my shoes, hurried out of my room, and ran down the stairs. I was still clamping my veil on my head when I caught up to the ranks about to enter the chapel. My sigh of relief caused a ripple of laughter at the end of the line and brought a look from Mother Forden. "Sorry, Mother," I whispered. She nodded toward my unbuttoned cuffs.

During lunch that day the nun in charge of Seven Dolors dormitory called me from the refectory. I had not put my bedspread on properly and left my nightclothes on the end of the bed. She stood in the doorway and watched as I remade my bed and folded my pajamas. When I looked to her for approval, she was gone. I wondered what to do next. Seek her out and try to explain? I rushed back downstairs to lunch. The tables were being cleared—late again.

If it is true that mortification brings enlightenment, the reaching rays of the sun should be resting on my head, like the picture of St. Paul's conversion in my fifth grade Bible history book. There are no beams of light. Nothing has touched my soul. I am filled with neither knowledge nor virtue. I do not feel the strength of the Lord surging through me. Should I have taken the time to fold my pajamas and put them under the pillow? Was being late for chapel a lesser crime? All the air is sucked out of me, and it is not over yet. I am about to learn there are consequences besides humiliation for not following the rules. All privileges are cancelled until I earn my *Très Bien* next Monday.

My mother had arranged for me to come home that weekend for my birthday. My sister would be home from college, and my friends had planned a get-together. I call my mother and fight back the tears as I try to express my embarrassment and my disappointment. She understands and is sorry for me. Thanksgiving is only two weeks away. You will be home for a week.

I hang up the phone, go to the dark corner of the chapel, and let the tears fall.

The Leaders

As harsh as the Sacred Heart system of discipline appeared, the rules relied more on pride than shame. There were awards and rewards that brought praise and stature.

From the very beginning, I kept my attention on the tall girls who wore the wide blue ribbons across their chests like young Olympians. They were poised and did everything Sacred Heart girls were supposed to do with an air of grace and sophistication.

They stood at the front of the ranks like soldiers ready to serve. If Mother Forden did not appear in the study hall on time, one of the blue ribbons would get us started. They were the worthy ones. The same ones who headed the clubs, captained the teams, and played the leading roles. They were the virtuous ones, the ones we should look up to. The ones who obeyed the rules and were never late.

The Marble Staircase

Just to the right inside the front door is a long parlor where one of the sisters, wearing a denim apron, moves silently among the furnishings, flicking a feather duster over tables and chairs. It is the same parlor where I was first welcomed to Eden Hall by Mother Benoist. This morning a bright sun beams through long windows, attempting to add warmth to petit point sofas, marble top tables, straight-backed chairs, and Oriental rugs. Our Lady's parlor is where an occasional visitor will sit and wait while Sister Portress summons the proper party. A series of bells brings a small black form gliding down the marble staircase where only the nuns' shoes tread. I can tell by the tilt of her head, and the way her habit riffles around her heels, it is Mother Benoist. I wonder who her visitor is, and why he has come with his attaché case in the middle of the week. Visitors are rare at Eden Hall.

Although we live under the same roof, we know almost nothing about the lives of these nuns we call Mother. Up the marble staircase they disappear, without leaving a trace, into a secret and sacred place where they live as a community. I imagine a long dormitory divided into cubicles, each containing a narrow bed covered with a white spread. A black crucifix hangs over the bed. There is a community room where a circle of wooden chairs awaits the nuns who will gather for spiritual reading and to do needlework and mend habits. A few religious pictures hang on the white walls, and the floor gleams yellow under the weakest beam of light.

The refectory where they take their meals is stark. Long wooden tables with benches are the only furnishings.

Who are these intellectual women who chose to leave home, family, and friends to join the Madams of the Sacred Heart and spend the rest of their lives separated from everyone except their community? Why did they give up every worldly comfort to live a life of poverty, chastity, and obedience? What did they mean by *being called?*

We do everything we can to learn about their secret lives. When one student discovers the nuns' long white nightgowns and little white bonnets hanging on a clothesline in a latticed enclosure, she can't wait to show us. My curiosity quickly overcomes a fleeting sense of shame. One has a red number inside the outline of a heart. A nametag? I calculate that number 23 is too short for Mother Stewart, Mother Carmody, or Reverend Mother Ashe. Too long for Mother Benoist or Mother Russell. Maybe Mother Forden.

Mother Forden is the nun we see the most. As *Surveillant* she is responsible not only for our discipline, but for our every move. With bell and clapper, she regulates our lives. I can't remember a morning when she wasn't there to start us on our way to the chapel, or a night she didn't clap us off to our dreams.

Mother Forden spends less time in the cloister than any of the other nuns, and I am certain she likes it that way. She seems worldlier than the others. She doesn't glide gracefully down the halls like Mother Benoist; her strides are long and purposeful and at times awkward. She is always adjusting her wimple to fit her heart-shaped face into the neat oval. Once when I was in her office, she climbed on a counter to reach something in cabinets hung so high I couldn't imagine what good they served. When she jumped down, her veil caught on something, and I feared for a moment that her coif was coming off. Her steely blue eyes can bring a whole school to attention, and a sprinkling of light freckles that spill irreverently on her sallow cheeks cancels any resemblance she might have to the saintly portraits I'd seen on holy cards. I can't picture her sitting in a circle doing needlework while Reverend Mother reads aloud from *The Lives of the Saints*.

Forden, as we refer to her privately, is the heartbeat of the school. She is always on the move, busy keeping us busy. Her energy is endless, and her creativity is contagious. There are always pageants to produce, plays to perform, songs to write, parties to plan: ice skating and hot chocolate at the pond, a valentine party to honor the Fourth Academic, or a surprise party in our room when she thinks we need a lift.

These special occasions always include food. Mother Forden has a weakness for secular food, and though we never see her indulge, we know she does, and we relish the thought of her downing a hoagie behind the closed door of her office.

Last-minute skits delight everyone at Eden Hall, and no one more than Mother Forden. When we host a hockey team from Stoneridge, the Sacred Heart school in Washington, D.C., we entertain them the night after the big game with a few skits we have gotten used to throwing together at the last minute. Black tights, black turtlenecks, a few strokes of white paint and presto, Yvonne I are skeletons. We fold ourselves into a dusty old trunk on the darkened stage in the gym and listen for the curtain to open. Then we wait for the music to begin—our cue to slowly raise the lid and exit the trunk. Before the first note is heard, Yvonne tries to muffle a sneeze. A giggling audience waits for whatever comes next. Under a single spotlight our slow and graceful emergence from the musty trunk turns into a tangled escape and a disjointed dance that bring laughter from the audience and a big smile from Forden.

There are always sets to be built, costumes to be created, a gym to be converted into a nightclub, and a study hall to be cleared. Moving two hundred desks out of the study hall for a pageant, and then moving them back into their perfect rows, is all part of the production.

Mother Forden helps me dress for the pageant on Saint Madeleine Sophie's feast day. The *congé* began with a late sleep and included games, a pageant, special *goûte* and, best of all, no classes. For the pageant I am dressed in the same simple habit that Madeleine Sophie and all the other Religious of the Sacred Heart have worn since she founded the order in Paris, 150 years ago. I am transformed in a graceful black robe and a thin black veil. I notice the fine weave of the material, and I wonder about the perfect fit. I am sure this garment belongs to one of the nuns, and I fear it may be one resting beneath a white cross.

Mother Forden leads me to a mirror as she is giving final instructions. I am first startled and then intrigued by my image framed in a white coif and wimple. I recognize only the eyes staring back at me. They are my mother's. Mother Forden pulls me away. Reverend Mother and the community arrive. The student body curtsies in perfect unison: subjects bowing to royalty. The readers take their places on stage. I adjust my sleeves, fold my hands at my waist, and wait in the wings.

After the pageant we all gather outside around trays of chocolate cakes. I glide down the path, enjoying the swish of my skirts, the click of the beads, and the laughter of my classmates. I am the tall dark dancer, my arms raised as if I can fly. Someone brings a camera out, and

I strike a reverent pose and then one not so reverent. Yvonne and I stroll down the path past the tennis courts, where two young boys grab the ball and run. I am in no hurry to trade these graceful garments for my baggy wool uniform.

When I finally go back inside, Mother Forden is working with the stage crew, clearing the stage. I go backstage to the greenroom, take a long last look in the mirror, and shed my elegant robes. Returning to the stage to help move a heavy platform and then taking up a broom to sweep the last scraps of the pageant, I notice the habit has disappeared. I picture it hanging in a closet somewhere at the top of the marble staircase.

The Mac Walk

In her novel *Frost in May,* Antonia White writes about her Sacred Heart school in Roehampton, England: "In its cold, clear atmosphere everything had a sharper outline than in the comfortable, shapeless, scrambling world outside."

At Eden Hall we enter and return from that scrambling, shapeless, outside world by way of a wide, tree-lined macadam path known as the Mac Walk. The walk runs straight from the circle in front of the mansion down along the hockey field and the pond before ending abruptly at the railroad tracks. There is no station, just a red and yellow sign nailed to a lean-to that reads TORRESDALE.

Legend has it that sixteen railway men stranded by the blizzard of 1888 were fed and given overnight lodging at Eden Hall. In return for the nuns' kindness, the railroad agreed to stop their trains to New York in Torresdale to board and discharge students leaving and returning from vacation.

On ordinary days the Mac Walk is a peaceful spot where nuns can be seen walking, reading their office, or praying their beads. In 1900 it was a promenade where young ladies including my grandmother took the fresh air in ankle-length black uniforms with high ruffled collars. Young ladies in those days got their exercise walking on the path.

The Mac Walk is our link between the medieval, cloistered world of Eden Hall and the other world outside the gates.

Today is a day of departure. By nine o'clock the path is alive with shouts of "Wait up!" "Have you got any cigarettes?" "Save me a seat!" "Are you going to New York?"

I drag my overstuffed suitcase, wondering why I brought all these clothes to Eden Hall in the first place.

"Hurry!"

"I'm coming!"

Passengers, surprised by the unscheduled stop, strain to see an army of young women inching their way toward an empty car. We crowd the window seats, mouthing good-byes to the nuns who have accompanied us to the tracks. Waving white handkerchiefs, they surrender us to that other world. While the train clicks away from the station, I press my cheek to the cold window, catching a last glimpse of the black silhouettes moving back up the path to a life they have promised never to leave. A moment of sadness evaporates. The tower clock disappears. "Who wants to go to the dining car?" A line of girls wearing knee socks, loafers, and fresh red lipstick lurches toward the front of the car.

We are passing through another world of small houses with drawn shades. Postage stamp lawns are covered with frost.

The conductor makes his way through clouds of cigarette smoke, clipping tickets and encouraging those in the aisle to be seated. At each stop there is a shuffling of suitcases and seats, cries of "Good-bye, have fun," and a last wave from the platform as the train pulls away.

My years at Eden Hall are to be filled with arrivals and departures moving from one world to the other, but some part of me is always left behind, like a ghost or a shadow waiting for a body to return and step back into that shadow. For now I catch my reflection in the window and see myself suspended between both worlds.

"Next stop, Trenton." The bridge is within sight. My mother is waiting.

Our return two weeks later finds the Mac Walk in a more subdued light. With the sun falling behind us, we follow our long shadows slowly up the path, reluctant to trade the smells of smoke and perfume for fresh polish and wax. Before complete darkness falls on the path, our skirts and sweater sets are packed away along with our worldly thoughts and pleasures.

It is our second night back after Christmas vacation when Yvonne tells me that, for some reason, one of her roommates will not be returning to Eden Hall. She suggests I move in with her and her other two roommates. That night, with reluctant permission, we are excused for the last few minutes of study hall to speak with Mother Forden.

We find her on her hands and knees, looking for something under her desk. "Can we help you, Mother?"

"Yes," she barks," move out of the light!"

I stagger back, knocking Yvonne into the hall. Brushing off her habit and straightening her veil, Mother puts whatever she retrieved on her desk and, without turning to face us, asks, "What is it?" I stumble through my request to vacate my cell in Seven Dolors and move into the empty bed in Yvonne's room. She turns and looks at me as if waiting for some further explanation. "After all," I say, "who wouldn't want to leave a place called Seven Dolors and move to one called Holy Angels?" She smiles and shakes her head. Although she doesn't mention my initial insistence about having my own room, I suppose that is what she is thinking. She nods her head and says, "Let Mother Carmody know, and ask her if it is all right with her if you move tonight."

"Thank you, Mother," we repeat several times as we back out of her office and make a dash up the stairs.

All my belongings are transferred in fifteen minutes down two hallways to a large square room with big windows and four closets. Mother Forden stops by to make sure I have arrived safely and everything is in order. Mother Carmody brings the holy water. We bless ourselves. I am welcomed in Holy Angels.

Day of Reckoning

The bell splits the silence before dawn, shattering the last fragments of a restless sleep. Dah-dong, dah-dong, dah-dong, dah-dong! A merciful pause—then four more clangs vibrate through a labyrinth of halls. The window is still dark. A whisper of fear moves me to cover my head with the pillow and lie still. The day has come, the day I have dreaded since my arrival. The day I had heard about before Eden Hall became a reality. The day veterans at Eden Hall refer to as the day of reckoning. The day is March 22, 1955, and I am about to face Oral Examinations.

Dies irae, dies illa

All week I prayed, "Lord, grant me some mysterious suffering, a fever, a concussion, anything that could turn this day of reckoning into a day in the infirmary. Gratefully will I accept any penance, and humbly will I submit to Miss Judd's cures."

I pick my head up and look around the room. No one is moving except Yvonne. She is shining her shoes. Cynthia and Kathleen are still in bed. I lie back down, close my eyes. My prayers have not been answered. Oh, God, I feel fine.

Requiem aeternam dona eis, Domine

Yvonne is always the first one up, and she is always smiling with her big white teeth. I look away, but she catches me. "Rise and shine," she says, holding up her gleaming brown oxford.

I shuffle to the sink. Cold linoleum seeps through the soles of my slippers. Warm water feels good on my wrists. In a minute Mother will come to the door with the holy water, and the day will begin. I enjoy the comfort of the warm water in the sink and let it run over my wrists. Before it overflows, I let the water out, and the word *catafalque* swirls out of the white enamel bowl.

Catafalque ... An open coffin rests on the draped catafalque in the middle aisle only inches from my shoulder. I see the dimly lit chapel, pews filled with uniformed girls in veils, surrounded by nuns kneeling in stalls under stained glass windows. A single bell tolls. Mother Forden swoops down the aisle, and in one quick motion removes a thin gold ring and a silver cross from the rigid body and pulls the lid down. Bang.

I gasp.

"What?" Yvonne says, startled.

"Nothing," I answer, and I listen to the rest of the water being sucked down the drain.

We dress in silence, buttoning starched blouses, straightening hose. The ten-minute bell rings. Yvonne is already on her way out the door. She stops and looks back at me sitting on my bed.

"I know," I say before she can say hurry.

"Reverend Mother," I curtsy, "I have question number three."

The question, typed on a long, narrow strip of paper, is drawn from a semicircle of eighteen identical papers arranged perfectly on a round silver tray. We each draw one. I stand alone, holding the paper in my white-gloved hands, staring at black letters. I squint them into focus.

Faceless shadows behind pleated white bonnets sit before me. Reverend Mother's chair is raised on a platform. Judge and jury wait. I open my mouth and then close it, lest some involuntary sound escape.

"Reverend Mother," I begin again. My blouse is wilting. "I have question number three." The student body holds its breath. A voice rises from my throat and begins to drone somewhere in the distance. The words from Scripture, tightly strung together, continue without pause or inflection.

"Thank you, Reverend Mother." I slip back into my seat and sit tall next to my classmates. My eyes focus clearly now on a perfect semicircle of shiny brown oxfords. The others are taking turns on the firing line. Yvonne has question number eight. Her voice is steady. Her blouse is crisp. She is a veteran.

Babies Were a Blessing

We had just settled into the big gray house on Ocean Avenue in Monmouth Beach for the summer. "Here they come," someone called. We ran outside and watched the car coming up the driveway. My father was bringing my mother and our new baby home from the hospital. It was Nanny's birthday, and when my mother placed the blue bundle in her arms and she proclaimed him "a fine-looking boy," I knew it was the best present she could have received.

We crowded around the bassinette to have a look at our new brother. I sat on the bed next to my mother and watched her lay out the ribbons from the flowers and gifts she received in the hospital. We would each choose a treasured satin bow or grosgrain ribbon, our reward for being good while she was gone. My mother had been gone for over two weeks. The doctors thought she needed a rest before bringing home her fifth child. I asked her if she liked the letter I sent her while she was in the hospital. Her eyes twinkled.

My summer would be different this year. I would be spending more time alone or with Nanny and my mother. My two sisters seemed to be growing up faster than I was. They now had their own friends and, because Kitty and Bobbie were my friends, I must not have bothered to make my own. I guess I was lonesome, but I wasn't unhappy. Most girls my age were playing with dolls. I had a real live baby. Nanny let me help with the feeding and bathing, and I walked proudly beside her when she wheeled him in the black pram covered with white *mosquito netting, and we stopped often to show him off to people who passed by and let them peer through the netting.*

By the next summer I would be pushing my brother, A.J. (Alexander Joseph, after my grandfather), in his blue metal stroller and walking him into town by myself. Our trip to the post office each morning, along the privet hedges laced with honeysuckle, was a sweet adventure.

The post office was a place of mystery. Envelopes fell down a slot and ended up in places like Chicago and New York. Nanny's blue tissue envelopes marked "air mail" made it all the way to England. The wooden floor creaked, and the ceiling fan wobbled, and everything smelled of brown paper and glue. I slipped my small envelope through the slot and watched it disappear. Mr. Wheeler had already distributed today's mail into lines of boxes whose gold-and-black-trimmed glass fronts filled two walls. When I dialed the secret code and emptied our mailbox, I could see all the way through to the back room. I spied on Mr. Wheeler stamping and stacking packages on a long table that held spools of string and rolls of brown tape. I spotted a radio and small coffeepot almost hidden by all the brown boxes. When I closed the box and it clicked shut, I turned to leave. Mrs. Wheeler was smiling at me, and I guessed she saw me spying, but I didn't think she knew that I was sending myself messages. Tomorrow I would return with my brother and pick up the envelope I had just mailed.

Years later when I read Eudora Welty's "Why I Live at the P.O.," I could smell the glue and brown paper and picture Mrs. Wheeler sleeping among the stacks of packages and making coffee in the morning in that little coffeepot.

Nanny was waiting for us when we got home from our walk. She took the baby, and I went to give my mother the mail. I could hear her making her daily phone call to her mother in New York: "Rheinlander 4-3779, please, operator ... Good Morning, Mother Honey." She called her "Mother Honey," but we called her "Dandy." All her grandchildren called her "Dandy" because she was. I left the mail on my mother's bed table and took my little white envelope to the back bedroom, climbed up on the bed, and took my time opening it. No one ever used the back bedroom or bathroom. By the end of the summer I had turned the shower in the adjoining bathroom into my clubhouse. On a white wooden stool I kept a collection of Archie comic books, several boxes of Chiclets that came two in a box, a jar of trinkets from Cracker Jacks or cereal boxes, and a cigar box filled with trading cards fastened into groups with rubber bands. All this was hidden behind a plain white shower curtain. No one ever visited my clubhouse, not even my sisters.

Today my mail included one of the trinkets from the glass jar and a note wishing me good luck in the swimming race on Saturday. There were only four swimmers in my age group, and I only had to beat one to get a medal.

My sister helped me out of the water at the end of the race. My mother said I was going faster than everyone before I swam into the sidewall of the pool. I went to the bathhouse and pressed the towel against my eyes.

Summer was almost over, and we were getting ready to go home to Berkeley Avenue, where the postman delivered the mail. We had to get ready before school started. Haircuts, new shoes ... the neighborhood would gather again in our front yard to play baseball. The Dodgers would be in another pennant race.

Maybe this would be their year.

And Then There Were Six

Our family seemed complete with three girls and two boys, and then after four years, she arrived on the summer solstice and was christened Charlotte Anne. Like the rest of us, she was named to honor someone who came before. Names were important. Katherine, Margaret, Elizabeth, Elliott, Alexander Joseph, and Charlotte Anne were names that tied us to our past. My mother was the only one in the family that called her by her given name.

She was as pretty and pink as any baby could be. Every night Kitty, Bobbie, and I took turns giving her the last bottle before she went to sleep for the night. Our days were spent at the beach club with our friends. When shadows of umbrellas leaned toward a dark ocean showing whitecaps, I knew it was close to four o'clock. I liked to beat my sisters home. I swung my leg over the seat and mounted my bike as if it were a horse, bumped over the curb, and pedaled nonstop until I skidded into the driveway, dropped my bike, and ran up the stairs. I peeked into the bassinette. She was sleeping. I traced one of her perfect hands with my finger.

By the end of the summer she held my finger in her hand and wouldn't let go.

When she was three I took her to Diamond's drugstore for an ice cream cone. Someone sitting at the counter asked her what her name was. Between licks of her cone as I pointed to the drips, she answered, "My mother calls me Charlotte Anne, my father calls me Tweetsie, my brothers call me Sherry, and Betty calls me 'get out of *my room.'" The story is often repeated, and the laughter is predictable. I laugh, too, but my heart is troubled.*

Now I call her Sherry Blueberry because I like the way it sounds, and it makes her smile. She says it doesn't matter how I spell her name: Sherry, Sherri, or Cheri.

I like hearing my mother call her Charlotte Anne. It sounds just right.

Another Departure

Departure day is still not easy.

My suitcase is almost packed. Uniforms, blouses, sheets, towels—where did I put those towels? Kitty and Bobbie will both be leaving for college next week. Bobbie hasn't talked much about going away to college. She, like my father, is a very good golfer. She once considered playing on the ladies professional tour; my father didn't approve. He said it was not a life for a girl her age, or something like that. To my knowledge, she never mentioned it again.

"What happens to a dream deferred?" Langston Hughes wondered.

Leaving will be easier this year. I know my place is waiting. New students will be finding their places soon, and like pieces in a puzzle they will fill in the ranks. Kathleen will be a new member of the Third Academic class, and she will fit into the puzzle.

I find my towels and dig in the back of the closet, looking for my brown oxfords. Eden Hall has given a whole new meaning to "rise and shine."

Kathleen slipped quietly into the ranks at Eden Hall and into my life. Her mother died when she was three. Her father and a bevy of aunts raised Kathleen and her younger brother: Aunt Katherine, Aunt Mary, Aunt Helen, and Aunt Ann. Dear Aunt Ann lived with the Rooney family. The others lived close by. There was Uncle Bill married to Aunt Katherine, and Uncle Slim married to Aunt Helen. I am not sure of any last names or how they were related, because they were just aunt and uncle from the day we were introduced. Cynthia, Yvonne, and I stormed into their lives, and they didn't seem to mind at all.

For our last two years at Eden Hall the Rooney home became our sanctuary in the outside world. While the other students would be staying at the Barclay Hotel on Rittenhouse Square, where our prom was being held, we chose to stay at Kathleen's.

Upstairs: Organdy, chiffon, and ruffles hung from curtain rods. We helped each other zip and fasten and took turns twisting in front of the mirror. Nail polish, hair spray, and perfume filled the air as we admired each other. "Time to go," Yvonne said, and we teetered down the stairs on high heels.

Downstairs: Mr. Rooney waited to greet our escorts, and the aunts and uncles were ready with cameras to record another event in Kathleen's life.

Outside: We posed in front of the azaleas. Red, purple, orange, and fuchsia pushed against each other. House after house, block after block, the neighborhood was afire with azaleas. A palpable excitement was growing as we posed for just one more picture.

Kathleen and I never dreamed how our friendship would grow over the years to include husbands and children and would last a lifetime. Even though we would both relocate several times, our paths kept crossing, and occasions would bring us together. We never questioned the synchronicity.

We stood as godparents for each other's children, cheered them on the fields. We went on ski trips together each winter and picked strawberries in the spring.

While Kathleen and I sliced, boiled, and waited for lids to pop, we listened to the children playing outside the kitchen window.

When I brought my first child home, she was there to coach me. In my darkest hour, when I rested my head in my arms, her hand was on my shoulder.

When she had some health problems and we couldn't see each other very often, we talked on the phone every day. The night before I went into the hospital for a back operation, she called me. "This time tomorrow it will be all over," she said. I thought about all she had been through and how brave she had been. I said good-bye. The phone call came while I was still in the hospital. She had made her final departure that night in her sleep.

For months I reached for the phone, and then I would remember.

The Dance of Faith

A slamming door and a rush of cold air announce Father Mackin's arrival in the sacristy each morning. Sister Sacristan has laid out the vestments: purple today, Lent, the season of penance.

Father Mackin, better known at Eden Hall as "Father Fleetwood," says Mass and gives communion to the entire community of religious and student body in less than half an hour. Everything about Father is built for speed: tall, thin, and straight as an arrow. He is a startling figure as he moves quickly and precisely on the altar. Genuflecting, stretching his arms wide, then hands closing in prayer, one movement flows into the next. Again and again he will become a living cross. His vestments sway as he moves from one side of the altar to the other and again when he turns to face the faithful. The altar boys kneel, stand, bow, and scurry to keep up.

"Introibo ad altari Dei."
I will go unto the altar of God.

"Ad Deum qui laetificat juventutem meam."
Unto God who giveth joy to my youth.

His deep voice fills the chapel. The altar boys respond in whispers. We follow the Latin words in our missals, careful not to drop any of the dozen holy cards tucked between tissue-thin pages. We confess our sins, proclaim our faith, ask for mercy, praise God, and at the sound of the bells come to our knees, proclaiming,

77

"Sanctus, Sanctus, Sanctus." We prepare for the mystery of bread and wine becoming the body and blood of Christ. Father holds the host high. Like flowers of the field, we lift our faces to the sun.

"Hoc est enim corpus meum."
This is my body.

Then he dips to his knee, his forehead resting on the altar. The same moves are repeated. The chalice is raised.

"Hoc est enim calix sanguinis mei."
This is my blood.

The nuns begin the procession to the altar. They come slowly, heads bent low, black veils falling over white wimples and hands tucked in wide sleeves, a procession of anonymous ravens.

We follow in our stiff white veils, hands together, pointed to heaven. We kneel at the altar. Father glides back and forth; the altar boy clings to his side with the gold plate.

When the Mass is over, Father Mackin is gone, out of the chapel, out of our lives, to some other life. We heard that he had been an Army chaplain during the war, which explains his speed and the deep lines in his face. A picture comes to mind of a younger man with thick dark hair and the same piercing blue eyes staring down the enemy while he ministers to a wounded soldier. I have seen chaplains in the war movies. How did this hero in fatigues and a metal helmet end up in a house full of women at a convent boarding school just outside Philadelphia?

Occasionally, Father stays to hear confession. I can see his silhouette on the other side of the screen, sitting sideways with his forehead resting in his hand. He never moves or twitches while I number my sins. The thought that he might be asleep crosses my mind. "For these and all the sins of my past life, I am truly sorry."

Father waves the sign of the cross and dismisses me to say my penance. I take my leave quickly while Father waits for the next sinner. My body feels light. My soul is clean.

Honor Code

Students in bathrobes carrying soap dishes, toothbrushes, towels thrown over a shoulder jockey for position at a long line of sinks. The mirror, running the length of the wall above the sinks, is covered in steam rising from bathtub cubicles. We clear circles with our hands and lean closer to inspect blemishes and apply cream.

At Eden Hall everything operates on a precise schedule. Bathing is no exception.

Three times a week, regardless of the weather, each student is allowed fifteen minutes to fill the tub, bathe, and leave the tub sparkling for the next person. We are also expected to act with honor, courtesy, and consideration for the next student. When it comes to the bathtubs, consideration for the next student in line has been consistently ignored by one of us.

On the appointed night, I watch in the mirror as the offended student reaches over the top of the cubicle; removes a towel, robe, and pajamas; and hurries down the hall to the laundry chute. We all exit the bathroom quickly and head down the hall. Before we get to our rooms, the wailing begins.

"Help, Mauther."

"Mauther, Mauther, they took my peyammas! Help, Mauther, my towel and my peyammas. They took them. Mauther, help."

Mother Carmody rises from her desk to investigate. We close our doors and wait.

We wait again for *Primes* on Monday morning. Someone, or perhaps all of us, will pay for the deed. Mother Forden reads from the book. "Fourth Academic, all very good. Third Academic," (we inhale) "all very good."

No wonder everyone loves Mother Carmody.

At home my bathtub was a place of retreat; a place to sequester myself from everything but the sound of water splashing into the deep, claw-footed tub. Warm water inched over my body and rose until I was completely covered in the warmth. Daydreams formed themselves like clouds and evaporated in the steam. When the water was at flood level, I reached with my wrinkled toes for the chain and pulled the plug to make way for more hot water.

The Shape of the Wimple

The news of changes being made at Eden Hall arrives in a letter before the summer officially begins. Mother Benoist is leaving Eden Hall and will be assigned to the other Sacred Heart school in the Philadelphia area known as Overbrook. In turn, Mother McDonnell, after thirteen years at Overbrook, will be the new Mistress General at Eden Hall. Because of the proximity of the two schools, Overbrook is our sister school and our chief rival. We play each other in basketball and hockey every year and consider our infamous battles on the court or field second only to the Army/Navy games. Even the nuns get involved in the spirit of these games. On one occasion Mother Forden passed out vitamin pills to the team the morning before a game, and another time she gave us the afternoon off from classes to rest before we boarded the bus and headed for City Line.

Next year Mother Benoist will be rooting for Overbrook. Could she really change allegiance that quickly?

These changes happen without warning at the determination of some higher authority. The nuns took vows of poverty, chastity, and obedience, and they obey without question.

At times there are disappointed students. The morning Mother "New Nun" left Eden Hall, the ground was still covered by snow. She stood in the driveway wrapped in a black knitted shawl, surrounded by the community of nuns. Mother "New Nun" was on her way to Rome to take her final vows and receive the silver cross she would wear the rest of her life as an outward sign of her fidelity. We huddled on the front porch, shivering in our blazers, singing a song of love and good wishes. At Eden Hall we write and sing songs for every occasion. We hurried back inside and watched from the windows as the station wagon with "Eden Hall" printed on the wooden door disappeared. The nuns, their arms tucked deep in their sleeves, stood silent, holding their memories of Rome close to their hearts.

There will be no send-off for Mother Benoist. She will be gone when we return to school. One face will take the place of another in the Mistress General's office. Mother Benoist and Mother McDonnell are the same dainty size and have the same quick step. Only the shape of the wimple will tell the difference from a distance—a more rounded look for the new Mistress General.

For me, the biggest change will be calling our new Mistress General "Mother McDonnell." She is and always has been Katherine to me. Not Aunt Katherine, just Katherine, my mother's younger sister and the third girl in a family of four girls. By the time I had reached the age of reason, she had entered the convent. Except for long trips for short visits with her while we were growing up, we never saw her. *Cloistered* was the word my mother used to explain why she never came to visit.

Her first year as Mistress General at Eden Hall is my last year. I will wear the first blue ribbon as head of the school and will have more contact with Katherine (Mother McDonnell) than most of the students. I know my mother is watching me closely as I read the letter, waiting for some reaction. "I hope she knows who's in charge," I say, handing the letter back. I hear her laughing as I hurry down the stairs. My sisters are waiting for me. I wonder how the other students will receive Mother McDonnell.

We drive over the bridge and down Ocean Avenue to the beach club, and I don't give it another thought. My head is filled with summer.

Meditation

Each morning Yvonne and I dress in darkness before the bell shakes the others awake. A few who belong, or aspire to belong, to the Children of Mary Sodality will spend some time in Mater's tiny chapel before Mass. We are new aspirants, and although there is no obligation to spend this time in meditation, I am honored to join the others.

The only light in the alcove off the main corridor illuminates a life-size painting of a young girl in a soft peach dress sitting with her eyes lowered and her hands resting in her lap. A beige mantle only partially covers gentle curls that touch her cheek and fall to her shoulders. A book and a sewing basket rest on the floor beside her, and on the other side a bright blue vase at her feet holds a single lily that is just beginning to bloom. She is called "Mater Admirabilis."

What is meditation? Some read from small books. Some hold rosary beads while others sit with their eyes closed. I kneel in the stillness, my eyes wide open, gazing at the picture alive under beams of light, and wait in faith.

Lily Procession

At Eden Hall we breathe our religion. It saturates our lives. Religious rituals bind us together. In pageants, plays, and processions, we carry on centuries-old traditions, none more solemn than the Lily Procession. On December 8, the feast of the Immaculate Conception, at Sacred Heart schools all over the world the same prayers are intoned, the same hymns are sung and the same ritual takes place. In Dublin, Roehampton, Marseille, Santiago, Tokyo, and Rome, young women consecrate themselves to the Virgin Mother, offering a lily as a sign of purity and devotion.

Dressed in our white Sunday uniforms and stiff white plumage, we make our way slowly through the hallways, our *a cappella* voices falling back on one another as we fill the empty pews. The nuns, already kneeling in their stalls, make a medieval picture awash in yellow light. The white altar gleams with golden vessels. The ciborium shines from its high niche. Priests in white vestments crowd the sanctuary, and altar boys in crisp surplices carry candles as tall as they are. The celebrants kneel, and the litany begins in a deep baritone.

> *"Sancta Maria."*
> We answer, *"Ora pro nobis."*
> *"Mater Christi."*
> *"Ora pro nobis."*
> *"Mater Admirabilis."*
> *"Ora pro nobis."*

The rhythmic chant moves back and forth, and our supplications rise on layers of incense that fill the chapel with a strong fragrance.

The organ brings us to our feet, urging our voices. The singing grows and swells with the volume of the organ until the sound reverberates from the vaulted ceilings.

One by one we move forward to present our lilies. "O Mary, I give you the lily of my heart; be thou its guardian forever." From generation to generation the words are the same. In 1900 my grandmother knelt at this same altar to pledge her fidelity, and years later my mother repeated the same petition. Today it is my turn. The words continue to punctuate the silence until the last student kneels and places her lily before the statue of the Blessed Mother. The organ comes alive again. It builds and builds, and our voices respond once more with a new energy. The wave of music rolls over me, filling me, lifting me up, and I know I am as close to heaven as I have ever been, and then it rolls again like thunder until the last voice and the last note end together in a breathless silence.

Everyone is waiting—waiting for the final dedication, the dedication that Mother Forden has written and I am to deliver in the name of the student body. For the past week I have practiced my delivery so it will be clear and then again so it will be smooth. I have recited the words for Mother Forden and have whispered them to myself. Religious dignitaries, the community of nuns, the students, alumnae, and visitors are waiting.

I move toward the heavy scent of lilies, carrying the red leather folder, and kneel before the Blessed Mother's altar. My gloves are damp. *I am five years old in a backyard procession. I hear Nanny saying, "Lovely."* The students sit behind me, shoulder to shoulder, row after row of white herons stretching their necks to see. Statues peer from pedestals.

A tear that never touches my cheek falls on the page. I begin, my voice weak, and when I try to increase the volume it begins to tremble. I take a shallow breath and continue. The words sound flat; I want to give them life. A feeling of panic is rising sentence by sentence. I try to swallow, and my throat constricts. My eyes travel the length of the second page. I cannot finish. I skip to the last paragraph and force out the rest of the words, ending with a weak "Amen."

Out in the hall I meet Mother Forden and hand her the folder. "I'm sorry, Mother. I don't know what happened."

She says something about not all of us being meant for public life. We are caught in a tangle of students heading downstairs to the refectory. I follow her to her office. She drops the red folder on her desk and picks up the clapper. I am waiting to hear more, but we walk down the stairs together in silence. On the last step I say I'm sorry again, and I take her smile as forgiveness. I am grateful that no one at our table tries to comfort me. I let the conversation move around me and listen to the smoothness in their voices. Soon it will be bedtime, lights out, darkness, blessed darkness.

Mystical Experience

A March wind lashes the chapel. Gusts rattle the red and blue saints. Sun floods through the west windows. Rafters are creaking, and something is floating and rocking and descending ever so slowly. I narrow my eyes, hold my breath, and nudge Kathleen. She follows my eyes to the vaulted ceiling and the floating object spinning sideways, appearing and disappearing through the shafts of sunlight. Benediction proceeds, and the wind continues. Incense is rising and swirling, and for a moment I can't locate it. I poke an elbow in Kathleen's side. The wind sounds like it is going to rip the roof off. The student body keeps repeating "pray for us" as the priest intones the novena. Is it my imagination, or is the "pray for us" getting louder as the windows rattle? Kathleen is looking up now. The wind outlasts the final prayers.

"Did you see it?"

She nods her head.

"Well?" I ask.

"A leaf," she says and smiles at my disappointment. Kathleen likes to keep me grounded.

Graduation Day

The day has arrived—a day we anticipated, looked forward to, and dared not think about. It has arrived just as I have pictured it, full of sunshine and singing birds that nudge me awake. I lie for a minute, listening. No more waking to that dreaded bell. The thought makes me want to wake the others before they are jarred from their dreams. Instead, I sit on the windowsill and watch the day beginning.

The morning passes quickly: Mass, breakfast, packing, yearbooks. After lunch we watch from the front porch as a parade of cars motor down the rarely traveled drive and park beside the hockey field, their shiny finishes gleaming under a high sun. Greetings, kisses, hugs, and the smell of tea and sweets fill the parlor, and then it is time.

We dress quietly among bulging suitcases, empty closets, and cleared bureau tops, helping each other with tiny covered buttons and ivy wreaths that need one more bobby pin. Sharing a single mirror, we bend and stand on tiptoe, checking one last time. "Don't forget your gloves." A quick look back at suitcases, discarded hangers, and empty closets, and we are clunking down the wooden staircase together to form ranks one last time.

Waiting in the chapel corridor for the organ to begin, a ripple of distress passes over me. Something isn't right. The familiar pews are filled with unfamiliar faces. The out-of-uniform people sit side by side in print dresses, flowered hats, dark suits, and silk ties. I spot my sister

Sherry in her yellow dotted swiss Easter dress, climbing over my father's legs to wave. I can't help waving back. Mother Forden would not approve. When I look for her, she is not beside us with her clapper. We are on our own.

The outside doors to the chapel stand open. The only other time I've seen these doors open was the morning they took the old nun's body out. It is exactly three o'clock. As the steeple bell rings, the organ begins with a roar. I have never seen the chapel so full of sunlight. We enter one at a time. Perfume and roses have replaced the cold, holy smells of candle wax and holy water.

A table in the middle aisle holds a stack of diplomas in red covers—our passports to the other world, where we will take our places as "valiant women" and perform our unknown roles in our homes and in society. We are ready to reenter that "warm, comfortable, shapeless world" and carve out our lives. Our time here is over.

Red, blue, and gold saints watch as usual. I wish these strangers could see the chapel at night, when a few vigil lights bring the statues to life and send shadows reaching across the mosaic tiles.

"Yvonne de la Chapelle Fulchiron ... Cynthia Barbara Rathbone ... Kathleen Patricia Rooney ... Elizabeth Elliott Shanley." I wonder if my grandmother is proud, hearing her name. We shared a special bond, not because of the name, but because I knew she enjoyed my company as much as I enjoyed hers.

We file across the loose mosaic tiles, carrying roses and diplomas, and out the doors into the warm sunlight, where the strangers look more familiar standing in family groups.

Sherry is pulling on my dress. "Wait," I tell her. I greet my grandmothers and Margaret Ann and receive congratulations. Margaret Ann is my friend. I didn't know she was coming. Our excitement erupts in squeals and laughter. We finish each other's sentences, as we always did. Sherry grabs hold of my hand, and I give in to her small fingers. We go inside; she wants to see my room.

Free from bells and clappers now, I walk through the halls and classrooms. I want to run down the glass corridor to the gym and slap the basketball on the shiny floor and listen for the cheers. I want to march up the marble staircase or just sit here alone in the empty study hall. Sherry is running up and down the aisles between the desks and has forgotten about my room. The sun is coming through the arched windows, making patterns on the yellow floor. I remember that first day and the patterns of sun in the hallway.

Back outside, I stop and stare; the groups are growing thinner, and my mother is talking to a woman holding a dog. I wonder if the dog was in the chapel. "Go find Mom," I tell Sherry, and she runs right past her. Cynthia is standing next to her father, and I realize the woman holding the dog is her mother. I don't see Margaret Ann.

Excited chatter is turning into good-byes. I haven't spent any time with my grandmothers, and I look for them. They are getting ready to leave. They are proud of me.

Cynthia and her parents are the first to depart. Her mother stands anxiously by the limousine, cradling the dog. Cynthia's father, with his silk handkerchief, engaging smile, and perfect mustache, ushers his daughter down the front steps and across the driveway to the car. She is the smiling heroine, and he is the handsome prince. We follow behind to bid our farewells. The prince makes an abbreviated bow and congratulates each of us again, then folds himself into the back seat.

We are blowing kisses, waving. My last image of Cynthia is sitting between her parents, still wearing her laurel wreath with that silly dog propped on her lap: a family portrait etched in happiness.

We will write. We will return, we will be friends, but we won't be roommates or desk mates or teammates. New students will fill our places at the round tables in the refectory. We won't even be pieces of pie.

We hurry back to our families. The crowds are beginning to thin. Time is passing so quickly.

I watch from the porch as the cars roll down the driveway.

Yvonne and I are spending the weekend at Kathleen's house. We have dates tonight with the boys we invited to our senior prom. Cynthia couldn't stay because they are leaving for California in a few days. California is a happy place for her. Her parents love to entertain, and there will be lots of parties and celebrities that she will never mention, and she will accompany her father on the road when he is doing summer stock.

We are the last to leave, and we linger as long as we can on the front porch, saying good-bye to the few nuns who remain. Our suitcases are packed in the trunk of my car, the top is down, and we are ready to go. I look for Mother Forden. Where is she? I don't remember seeing her from the time we left the study hall and processed toward the chapel. She had not been there beside me as we waited for the organ to begin.

I need to say good-bye. I go back inside and run past her empty office. The halls are empty, and there is no sign that anything special happened here today. Kathleen and Yvonne are waiting.

We drive through the stone pillars as the sun is going down. Yvonne and Kathleen wave bouquets of roses. *Graduation ... salutation ... jubilation.* Words tumble through my head.

Time passes. Listen. Time passes.
—Dylan Thomas, *Under Milk Wood*

We went separate ways, followed different paths, and tried to stay in touch. We ran and stumbled in a hurry to grow up. We cheered each other's successes and shared each other's pain. When Cynthia's father died suddenly of a heart attack, her pain was great. She was now living at home, taking care of her mother, who was ailing. Because we hadn't been in touch for quite a while, I was surprised when her call came to say she was coming to Maryland to visit her godmother. Had I heard of Rosa Ponselle?

"Rosa Ponselle, the opera singer, is your godmother?"

We kept interrupting each other. "Go ahead; no, you go," we laughed. She sounded excited, and so was I. How was she? What was she doing? How was her mother? Had I heard from Kathleen or Yvonne? I tried to feel her life as we talked. The trip was important. It would be a break. There was a sense of urgency in her voice. Before we could make our plans, her mother's voice came across the line. "Cynthia dear"—"Yes, Mother." "Cynthia dear, I need you."

"Yes, Mother, I'll be there in a minute." She sighed and laughed again. I pictured her mother propped on a cloud of pillows, the dog nestled beside her.

"Sorry," she said, and promised to call again soon.

Soon, I repeated as I hung up the phone and sat looking out the window at a warm autumn day ready to take its leave. I listened to the children's voices outside.

How would Cynthia view our country living? How would she take to our boys? They would surely take her by the hand and lead her into the woods to view their latest tree house. No sooner had we admired their first tree house than they found a better tree. Down came the first, and up went another. Pounds of nails marked a trail through the woods. The builders were learning their trade.

They often returned from the woods with treasure. They cried when we let the box turtle go after twenty-four hours in a box. A small white milk snake would spend the night in a glass jar on the back porch, but the day I discovered the boys in the kitchen sharing cookies with our Shetland pony, Touchy, I had to put my foot down. "No ponies in the kitchen!" I declared.

Cynthia's call never came.

The call that came was from Yvonne.

Three lines of print in the *New York Times* reported Cynthia Barbara Rathbone ... age thirty ... daughter of Basil Rathbone ... died suddenly ...

No one's life is that small.

Why? Yvonne and I asked each other. How?

There would be no answers.

Listen. Time passes.

Summer lures us back to the Jersey Shore. Like migrating birds, we return each June to the barrier island and our home at the end of the lagoon.

While the children run to find their bikes, we stretch our legs and fill our lungs with salt air, checking to see how the house stood up against winter. On summer mornings sunshine knocks on the windows, and we wake to the sound of gulls. I open the windows wide.

The shrill "kyew, kyew" of the osprey announces their earlier arrival. They are already repairing last year's nest. This summer we will watch for two or maybe three unfinished chicks poking their fuzzy heads above the nest, looking more fragile than newborn babies. Toward summer's end we will watch the fledglings take flight and, if we are lucky, spy the young ones learning to hunt: folding wings and diving like some feathered bomb, feet first into the sea, hoping to snatch a fish in its talons. It is hard to tell if they are serious about fishing or just having fun doing cannonballs, producing nothing but splash.

Change happens slowly on this island. The marshlands don't turn green with the first warm rain. They stretch and rise from a tight tangle of roots under winter's mat of brown grasses. Before there is any sign of conversion, the soft velvet air and the smell of sunshine assure me winter has worn itself out.

We live here in nature's time: sunrise, high tide, low tide. We tell time by the slant of light. The turtles come ashore to lay their eggs in June. In July we watch the osprey fishing and feeding their babies. The ocean temperatures are warmer, and we trek over the dunes to ride the waves. Early in August the "school birds" line the telephone wires. They come to feed on the ripe bayberries. We call them school birds because they remind us that summer is passing. The birds swoop down with a loud whir of wings and disappear into bushes that tremble as fruit is plucked from their branches. They exit with round little bellies and circle back to perch on the black wires. In a few days they disappear, leaving purple-stained sidewalks.

Days slip away like tiny sea creatures that slide through my fingers as I stroke my way through the bay. I like to swim backstroke with the sun on my face and cool currents moving beneath me. Resting on the warm wooden dock, I listen.

A fish jumps: splash. My eye is not quick enough. I wait, watching the widening rings, hoping to catch a jackknifing flash of silver. There is another splash and another set of rings. So much happens just below the surface. A heron wades and waits.

Thoughts meander on the river. Past and present wash together on some inexorable tide.

I can go to the river that winds through the country-side, cuts through flat farmlands, shoulders past rocky cliffs, horseshoes, straightens, and bends again. In summer children are stretched across black inner tubes, laughing and calling to each other as they bump through shallow waters across the stones. The river bubbles and spins them downstream to a deep pool, where they slip out of their tubes and submerge into the cool darkness, resurfacing sleek and shiny.

Another time there is only a young boy fishing; his dog waits on the bank while the boy moves skillfully from rock to rock. He seems never to tire of flicking and reeling in his line. When a small rainbow fish glistens metallic in the sun, the boy struggles to remove the hook, then frees the fish downstream. The dog runs to fetch it and stops in the shallows puzzled, then returns to the boy re-worming his hook. They wade back in the water together.

This is not the forbidden river of my childhood, the deep river at the end of the road where I dare not linger for fear of fishermen inside the shack. Bleached red-bottomed boats surround the shack, barely visible in a low, gray winter sky. I watch from hiding for the stream of black smoke, the only clue that there is life behind the boarded windows.

When the summer people arrive, another layer of yellow stones has been dumped and spread so thick that our bikes skid and we jump off. Yellow stones are smooth, and we can walk across them barefoot even in the beginning of the summer. The shack has been painted, and the door stands wide open. The screen door bangs closed as fishermen and boat owners come and go. From the dock I can see the big red Coke box that holds two large blocks of ice and green bottles floating in the melt. My arm goes numb to the elbow, reaching for the sculpted bottle. I close the lid, stand my prize on the top, wipe my hand on my shorts, and take three tries at the rusty opener before a whoosh of brown bubbles covers my hand. I suck the bubbles, leave my sticky dime on the box, and run back down the dock to my brother.

If I return to that river today, on a sparkling September morning, all the clean boats will be tucked in their slips. Their gold names swim in the reflection of the sun. The shack is gone, and so are the yellow stones. A high-rise building with matching balconies looms over landscaped paths leading to the docks. But if I take a rowboat out past the first channel marker and turn into the shallow waters that cut through the marshlands, I can sit hidden by the grasses and watch the same sunsets.

Schools of tiny fish flick back and forth beside the dock, shining in the sun like treasure. We call them killifish or mummy chugs. We are not sure which they are, but we like saying both names. Do the children remember catching them in a yellow bucket? The tiny fish lost their shine in a bucket. We poured them back into the lagoon.

On this small barrier island we are never far from the sea and always aware of its presence. Sometimes the ocean leans in gently on afternoon mists that sweep across the dunes. When the wind is right and the surf is up, we are drawn by the sound of curling, crashing waves that toss shells up on the beach. Shells we will pick up in the morning before the sea reclaims them. On calm, sunny days at low tide we listen to small waves slap the beach and sizzle up the sand.

Listen.

When you grow up in a large Irish family, you learn early on how to listen. I was born at a time when families sat around the dining room table to eat and then listened to the radio—"We have nothing to fear ..." At wakes and weddings or any large gathering of family, we listened to stories. The stories, the wonderful stories, told and retold.

After the hugs and hellos, the rites of holding new babies and squeezing their hands, the great kitchen confab and the magical meal, we all settle down for the stories. *Remember* rises from steaming coffee mugs and floats around the room. The children sit quietly for the first time all day. The stories may begin in the present but invariably move back to a black and white past. The storytellers take turns, and the listeners keep them close to the facts. Sometimes it is hard to separate fact from fiction, but it doesn't matter. We listen, we laugh, we learn. Some of the older children will notice that over the years a story may change, depending on the teller. Can the children hear the longing behind the laughter?

What do I really remember? I remember a green and white striped dress, berry picking with my sisters on a sandy path, the sweet musty smell of a summer cottage, my grandmother standing tall on long porch lined with rocking chairs. Her arms outstretched, "The children," she says. We were the children once. Now we are the storytellers, piecing together the past.

The bells are ringing. They ring the Angelus every day at noon. The sound floats up the lagoon.

At Eden Hall we stood behind our chairs in the refectory before lunch and prayed. "The angel of the Lord declared unto Mary ..." I hear the clear voices of the children. "Hail Mary, full of grace ..."

Listen. Time passes.

On the night before her fifth birthday, as I tucked my daughter into bed, she began to cry. "I don't want to be five. I like being four." I wiped her tears. My own childhood fear was that I would wake up one morning and things would be different and never as good.

Change shouldn't happen overnight. Every good author gives hints, so as not to catch the reader completely by surprise.

Was I not paying attention? Was there talk of change behind cloister doors? The changes came like a bolt of lightening without any warning or thunder.

Dust had settled on the throne of Saint Peter. It was time to open the windows and let in some fresh air. When the windows were open, the winds blew and dust flew.

At the Sacred Heart motherhouse in Rome, delegates arrived from around the world to decide how their order would implement this call for change and still remain true to the principles of their founder, Saint Madeleine Sophie Barat. The word reform *echoed throughout the conference.*

No longer would "Pater noster, qui es in caelis" be intoned in the Catholic Church. No longer would "Dominus vobiscum" fill the nave, giving rise to the congregation's "Et cum spiritu tuo." No more round Latin words sweet and smooth in my mouth like peaches. How would I praise God in an everyday language?

Cloister became part of the past; mothers became sisters, and more than a few stepped away from teaching to respond to the needs of the poor. They went where needed: projects, hospitals, and third world countries. Flowing black habits became a sign of the past. God was calling them to a different way. Many hurried to answer the call. Some would live in small communities; prayer life was on their own. Within months, Mother McDonnell became Sister Kate and was living in a project in Washington, D.C., with a group of five nuns from various apostolic orders who found their ministries with the sick, the poor, the homeless, the abused. For them this was a time of faith, a time they believed was overdue.

For others who wanted to lead the traditional religious life, this was a time of turbulence, a time of questioning. From the day they took the vows of poverty, chastity, obedience, these nuns had learned to obey their superiors and not to question. Now there were many questions. What about the lives they had been living? What about the rule of Saint Madeleine Sophie? What did it mean now to be a Religious of the Sacred Heart?

There was no time for mourning; the old order was gone. Some of the religious continued their lives of teaching while adapting to the changes. Others hesitated and tried to hold on. Some got lost in between and left the convent.

Mother Forden was one of them.

When news came that Eden Hall would be closing its doors, students, teachers, parents, and alumnae were shocked. Committees were formed, alternatives were offered, and appeals were made. Word came from the motherhouse in Rome. The decision was final.

Clouds formed. Thunder rumbled.

We used to bundle on the sofa when the storms woke us during the night. From the end of the lagoon we watched the dark clouds move out to sea. The lightning made us blink, and we exclaimed with every crash of thunder. We knew when we returned to our pillows that tomorrow we would find the air swept clean.

How do you explain to a four-year-old that we cannot stop time or even slow it down? All we can do is try to keep our balance.

Time.

The Greeks had two words for time: *chronos* and *kairos.*

Chronos refers to the time we can measure. It is the past going through the present and into the future. Yesterday is today's memory. Tomorrow is today's dream. Memories pass through the present, and we carry them into the future.

Time passed slowly when we were eager to grow up. Now we ask, "Where did time go?"

Kairos is the now, the instant that is a swift, indecipherable passage from this to that.

Kairos is in God's time—a time that has no beginning and no end. It cannot be measured.

Kairos is the everlasting now. Eternity?

There was a time when the field was there. You could depend on it. Set between a stone farmhouse and outbuildings on one side and a tangle of woods on the other, the field lay. New green in the spring, deepening to a cool evergreen in the summer, it grew tall with corn. Behind the field was a wooded ridge; before it wound a narrow country road.

As long as I can remember, the field was there, each season bringing a new beginning.

By mid-August the corn tasseled, and the first shades of brown appeared. Soon the woods were on fire in autumn reds. Thinning rows of dry, colorless corn waited for the coming of the combine. Geese foraged the stubble and flew north in uneven formations. Snow brought silence to the field. A few broken stalks poked through the white crust—reminders of seasons past.

Every season the field was there, a framed miniature of the countryside. Each day it sheltered groundhogs and pheasants. At night it fed deer.

Then one day they arrived. Giant yellow earthmovers stood silent on the slope overlooking the field. A disjointed orange backhoe, a flatbed truck, and a quilted trailer would follow and park next to the road. The field was surrounded. One morning, about the time of the first frost, the earth trembled and the rumble of engines decreed the death of the field.

In a matter of days the ground was mounded and flattened, shaped and reshaped, and when the veil of dust settled, the field was gone.

Huge oak trees that grew for over a hundred years were felled in a matter of hours, their wood gathered by neighbors and stacked against winter. Some have already forgotten the way their gnarled roots gripped the bank along the road.

One spring morning while walking in the field, our untrained retriever startled me by flushing a nest of pheasants.

He bounded, ears up and flopping, into the field, stopped, pointed, and then bounded again. In a burst of squawking and a great rustle of wings, the birds took flight. Barney cocked his head, as if unsure of what he had done and what he should do next. "Here, Barn," I called, and he trotted to my side while the pheasants glided serenely out of reach.

The bulldozers could not be called off. They continued day after day, blowing black smoke until there was no trace of the field's rolling contour. Deep, disturbing treads replaced familiar tractor treads. Animals retreated deeper into the woods. The cardinal deserted the lilac bush.

Now long lines of yellow buses come each day, and the children raise the school yard flag: the sign of a new beginning. They sit at new desks in a sleek, low brick building, while a red fox paces the fence line in front of the woods, searching out some old den or, perhaps, protecting a new one.

> To the attentive eye, each moment of the year has its own beauty, and in the same field, it beholds, every hour, a picture which was never seen before, and which shall never be seen again.
> —Ralph Waldo Emerson

Time passes. Listen. Time passes.

They're home now. They return from college, carrying bags full of laundry and wearing newfound philosophies. We listen, their dad and I, and we smile. *It's okay,* we say.

We watch an earring appear and then disappear and a full head of hair turn to a shiny pate. When they are all home at once, the shower runs continually.

The phone rings constantly, and the house vibrates with their music. Running shoes and sneakers fill the hallway, and the living room lamp wears a baseball hat.

They come and go all day, and at night I listen for their return.

The red eye of the clock reads 2:00 a.m. The cars are all in the driveway. I slip back into my empty space and listen to the steady breathing beside me. "They're home," I whisper and sink into my pillow.

Soon they are gone again.

Bedrooms yawn emptiness. Stillness settles over cleared bureau tops. The cat, wrapped in its tail, sleeps in a patch of sunlight on the bed. The steady heartbeat of the grandfather clock fills the house. Outside, a woodpecker hidden in foliage hammers a tree in the woods.

We await the children's return and prepare for their leaving.

Listen.

A train whistle fades in the distance.

I am on my way to the motherhouse in Albany, New York, where the nuns now live in retirement. Sister Kate was not ready to retire, but it was time. I sit on the left-hand side of the coach and watch for the familiar landmarks.

The train doesn't stop there anymore. It doesn't even slow down. The engineer blows the whistle, and the train rushes past the red and yellow sign that is just a blur.

The train to New York doesn't stop in Torresdale because Eden Hall is gone: the dormitories, the gym, the music room with the red and white checked floor where Anna Maria played the piano and we learned to sing Spanish songs and to dance the cha-cha.

When the school was gone and the chapel stood alone, I could catch a glimpse of the steeple if I was on guard. The chapel is gone now, too. The historic chapel, the first consecrated chapel in the United States, which stood for almost one hundred and fifty years, could not be saved. The dioceses, committees, individuals, and finally the firemen, could not save it.

In early morning darkness, before the sun brought life to the red and blue saints and the high, sweet note of Gregorian chant still lingered in the air, we filled the gleaming pews and waited. The white altar sparkled in candlelight. The sanctuary bell often caught me by surprise, and I had my second awakening of the day. Enter the priest, followed by the altar boy. The round Latin words filled my mouth and rolled off my tongue.

At Eden Hall we used to ride the slow train (the local) on a few Saturdays when we had permission to go to Philadelphia. We hurried down the Mac Walk dressed in our "civies" to catch the local arriving at 30th Street Station before the city was wide awake. Huddled outside Wanamaker's, we shared stale cigarettes and tried to keep warm while we waited for the doors to open. Anyone who wanted to go to Tourmalinos for lunch should meet at the Golden Eagle by eleven o'clock.

Strolling arm in arm down the sunny side of Chest-
nut Street, a chorus line of polo coats and striped
scarves, we scattered pigeons and surprised shoppers.
When we arrived, the waiters were still spreading white
tablecloths. We crowded around the entrance and com-
pared our purchases. "Look," I said, pulling a pair of
extra long knee socks out of my bag, "for tall girls."
  By four o'clock we were back on the train, the art
museum and boathouses falling behind us with the sun.
At five fifteen we were in uniform and late for study hall.
Mother Forden waited impatiently in the doorway. She
did not look happy. We entered quickly ... with red lips,
our hair carrying the smell of smoke.

When I arrive at Kenwood and see the tiny figure
waiting at the end of the long hallway, I know it is Kate
and move quickly past empty parlors. Giving her a hug,
I feel her fragile body. "I am fine," she says. She holds
me at arm's length and looks up at me. Is she looking
for the girl she remembers at Eden Hall? I hug her more
gently this time.

Kenwood was once a thriving school, as well as
the novitiate where Katherine came in faith as a young
woman to dedicate her life to God.

Up a flight of stairs—she doesn't need the elevator—
she leads me to my room. I look at a line of closed doors
with names written in perfect calligraphy. *Betty Shanley*
is written on my door. Has she forgotten my married
name, or is this a kindness to make me feel at home? I
like being that girl again, even for just a minute, before
I realize I will be sleeping in what used to be the cloister.
  A narrow bed, a small desk, a wooden crucifix, and
a window overlooking the paths she walked and prayed

as a novice. She was wearing a white veil then. After a year of contemplation, she would take her first vows and receive the black veil.

She tells me again that she is fine. She spends her days in the chapel and assisting some of the older ones in the infirmary. The food is wonderful. She will introduce me to the chef. She tells me all about his family and asks about my children. She can't remember their names.

"I have trouble remembering names," she says.

"I have trouble, too," I assure her, "but you nuns are lucky; you just call each other sister." Her laughter rings down the empty hall.

She misses being outside. "They don't like to go outside much." I promise we will walk tomorrow.

Up a steep hill to the cemetery, visiting the dark ornate crosses naming the nuns who lived in the eighteen hundreds, and then back to the small white grave markers of those I know. Reverend Mother Barry, Mother Benoist, Mother Carmody ... "This is where I will rest one day," she tells me.

Walking back down, the sun is bright, and it is hot. We stop under a huge oak and look up at a tree that is hiding what I think is a mockingbird. She gets dizzy and I grab her hand, and we continue.

I sense her reluctance to go back inside. We sit in the shade of morning sun and remember. It is a happy childhood that she recalls: roller-skating in Central Park with her sisters, going to dances—she loved to dance. She recalls the early morning Mass after a New Year's Eve party, when she heard God's call and her parents' reaction. Surprised ... and completely supportive ... she should wait and pray until she was sure. She can't remember how long she waited. I ask about Mother Mejia, who is also living here.

Madre, as we all called her, did not usually teach but was called into service. Because of a schedule conflict, I was unable to take French, the language all Sacred Heart students take pride in understanding. I was the only student at Eden Hall studying Spanish.

We met for our lessons at one end of Our Lady's parlor in a museum-like setting and sat in antique arm chairs covered with hours and hours of needlework. Above us hung a large oil painting of entwined bodies with transparent wings, rising out of a dark place, entrapped in an ornate gold frame.

While I learned Spanish, Madre learned about my American childhood.

She was amazed at the freedom I had growing up. I told her about playing football with the boys on Clairmont Terrace. I told her about spending months in bed with a sinus infection. I even confided in her how, when my mother came into my room in the middle of the night to give me my medicine and refill the steam kettle and then felt my forehead and asked if I wanted anything, I wished she would stay for a while. I never said anything. She said "God bless" and shut the door, and I fell back to sleep.

I wanted to know about Madre's life. Did she have any sisters? Did she ever build forts or take dance lessons? Did she ever have a boyfriend? When and why did she leave her country? I knew not to ask.

In the morning on the way to the chapel for Mass, I see a nurse wheeling Madre toward the chapel. I hurry to catch up. "Madre," I say.

"Sister Serita," she says. We are all sisters now. I bend down and tell her, "I am Betty Shanley; you taught me at Eden Hall."

"I know who you are," she says, but there is no sign that she does. "I'm in a hurry," she says. I recognize she has suffered a stroke. Another sister shuffling down the hall greets me with a hug, and Madre disappears around a corner.

I watch her across the chapel as the young priest talks directly to the nuns about the power they have in the eyes of God. The power they have in this world, in this place, in this moment. These women who have given up their lives and now have lost control of their bodies are nodding their heads *yes*. Some are smiling. Their faith is unwavering. They are living in God's time.

Some of the younger nuns who come to visit on Sundays join us for breakfast. Katherine is right. The food is delicious. She wants to know all about the work the nuns are doing. While they are talking, I slip away. I want to see Madre before I leave.

I find my way to the infirmary. The bed rails are up. She is safe, sleeping under a pink blanket. I watch her sleep. I want to touch her hand but am afraid it might wake her. I recall her sweet and humble demeanor and whisper, *good-bye, Madre.*

I should have come sooner.

Katherine's small hand feels warm in mine. We walk slowly toward the front door. I hug her gently and whisper good-bye.

The winds of change blow softly now.

Time passes.

Someone needs to know that once upon a time there was a school called Eden Hall and a chapel that was always warm, and red and blue saints came alive each morning in the rising sun. A place where dedicated nuns, whom we called *Mother,* spent their lives doing God's work and providing young women with an elegant education. Someone needs to know about this time and place that will never be seen again.

Amen. Amen.

Note

*Sometimes when we are young
we come into a world that seems the
whole of human experience. Beauty
and mystery are there. Energy and effort,
camaraderie and newness are there.
We come into a new place, stepping away
from all that was familiar and known,
into a company of strangers who become
a band of friends kept for a lifetime.
The order and discipline of the place
expands our sense of freedom to choose
our way amid a new and higher order
of things. Our being breathes deeply of
honor and courage, pleasure and wonder,
reverence. Our thought deepens,
our feelings awake to wide vitality.
Our hopes rise daily like the sun shining
over the playing fields, glistening across
pathways to here and there, glancing
off the treetops in the distance to
drop like warm color over everything
at the end of the day.*

*Eden Hall was a place like that.
And more.*

j.t.

Acknowledgments

To all the dedicated nuns and teachers who over the years instilled in me a love for learning and whose example I drew on during my years of teaching, I have been blessed to have had so many of you in my life.

Thank you, Josephine Trusehler, for being my teacher, my mentor, and my gentle friend. Jo, you are my North Star.

Thank you to my daughter, Shanley Driscoll, for the many readings, your good suggestions and, of course, your technical advice.

Thank you, Henriette Leanos, my classmate and friend, for your understanding that kept me going when I doubted, and for introducing me to Laura Oliver.

Thank you, Laura. You are an inspiration.

Special thanks to my friend, Louise Hatch, for all the happiness and laughter you have added to my life. You shared so much of this memoir.

How do you thank a husband who has encouraged me in everything I have attempted in my life and has always been my biggest fan?

Elizabeth Driscoll

ENFANT DU SACRÉ COEUR

EST ANCIEN/NE ÉLÈVE DE
NOTRE MAISON

A *Stuart Country Day School Princeton NJ USA*

DIRECTEUR *Frances de la Chapelle RSCJ*

2008

Sacred Heart schools today flourish in the United
States, and in forty-three countries around the world.
Alumnae are welcome at any of these houses, and
when they visit they will know they are home.

18674380R00076

Made in the USA
Middletown, DE
16 March 2015